Virtual Education

Dimensions of Educational Resources

V.T. Patil

AUTHORSPRESS

Worldwide Circulation through Authorspress Global Network
First Published 2002
by Authorspress

E-35/103, Jawahar Park,
Laxmi Nagar, Delhi-110 092

e-mail: authorspress@yahoo.com
quantum_soul@mantramail.com

Typeset in NewCenturySchlbk by Chitra Computers

Virtual Education: Dimensions of Educational Resources
ISBN 81-7273-084-5

Printed in India at Tarun Offset, Delhi.

Preface

The development of computer-based technologies has revolutionised teaching and learning process. Today, as we stand on the threshold of the third millennium the advent of virtual classrooms and video-desktop technologies promises interesting possibilities, including the remerger of the formal and informal streams. Education is now available anyplace, anytime and anywhere through web-based virtual learning centres. These centres are allowing professionals from a wide variety of institutions, the opportunity to maintain a competitive edge in their careers through classes and workshops.

Virtual education is essentially the education that takes place over the internet using a computer interface. It allows users to learn information from any location that has internet access. There are many other forms of distance learning, such as real time audio, interactive-video and written materials and it provides the user with the unique ability to interact with both the professor and other students while learning the material at the same time. It also provides the convenience of taking courses when you have time to fit them into your schedule.

Virtual education provides the added benefit of easily updating course material as new information is made available. Most other forms of traditional learning have prohibitive costs that make it difficult to constantly update and revise their product. This allows e-learning providers the ability to constantly revise their product based on feedback from their customers and changes in the marketplace.

In recent years, with the improvement in network capabilities and course content, online education is becoming a viable alternative to taking courses in the classroom. Not only does online education provide a relative price advantage but it also provides a wide range of course materials. Coursework offerings range from professional growth to on-the-job training. Programmes can often be tailored to meet the specific needs of an organisation at the given time they choose to participate. This coursework gives brokers the opportunity to continually build on education and training. It can provide a useful opportunity to add a new business strategy to address any recent developments. Online education can also help to enhance current business strategies by providing new ideas or opportunities to brainstorm.

This study is a serious attempt to come to grips with a contemporaneous subject of immense significance and relevance in the IT driven revolution of the Third Millennium.

The author is grateful to K Cherry Sudarshan for his diligence and interest in getting the copy ready for the press at the earliest.

V T Patil

Contents

1
Virtual Reality in Education

This is age of virtual reality (VR) concept. The concept has emerged and stands as the vanguard of a new technological revolution. Whether creating new worlds, or recreating 'real world' environments, VR technology is likely to have a major impact on the future of education. It may potentially redefine the system of education as we understand it today.

Technology of virtual reality is a regime which requires its own education. To participate in this culture in any way means acquiring an almost scholarly literacy. One must be able to read and write unambiguously, search efficiently and methodically for information, and then interpret it precisely and coherently. The traditional sources and instruments of power in the real world are in the virtual real world replaced with information. When we learn to revise our experience by learning to operate in virtual reality, we also become citizens of that regime. Those who do not have access to this technology or fail to commit themselves to the particular kind of learning it insinuates are the underclass of the regime.

E-mail, the basic means of digitally mediated distance learning, is rapid, variably asynchronous, epistolary communication. Having constructed thoughts and images into words and graphics, and those into digitised data, we send them off to a recipient who reverses the construction. As though to recover the personal or the confiding nature of old fashioned letter writing, we who frequently depend upon the artifice of e-mail can readily observe how even the very business-like exchanges between teachers and students in distance education become confessional. As easily as we can be confessional on e-mail, we can lie. When receiving a heart-catching statement from someone whom we know nowhere but in virtual reality, we can not judge its sincerity, any more than we can tell if the e-mailed work of virtual students is authentically theirs.

The state of nature in virtual reality, a nature so entirely comprised of information, forces us to be uncertain about the truth. Perhaps we long to receive from a distant student or colleague a bit of handwriting, the feel of a handshake, a shift of posture, a quick grimace or flutter of eyes, even an odour of stale tobacco. We look for something that betrays the unconstructed presence of another person. Even as we move headlong into total immersion, we want something inaccessible to digits.

Words, sounds, 3-D images, motion, and even smells and the feel of surfaces — all of these can now be melted into data streams. Soon no doubt, taste, balance and proprioception will follow. These challenges are mere technical problems. We know that once the given has been liquefied into data, the stream can be channelled, sorted, and temporarily frozen into any appearance one chooses. In the online chat rooms, these constructed presentations of self are rightly called *avatars*. In such a world, teachers can programme their avatars to lecture and to test; teachers need not be authentically present at all.

The future of virtual reality in education is like sculpting fog, but there are definite pressures that will bring virtual reality to education in the near future. There are many types of virtual reality systems. The typical reaction to what is virtual reality can be summed up in the image of immersion. The user of the system must have a feeling of being somewhere else. The other types of altered realities include "cab simulators" which is generally reserved for flight, military, and entertainment use where the user is enclosed in a platform which simulates a place, such as a fighter plane, that is fed pictures that induces the user to think they are in the simulation of flying or driving a tank. Projected displays are huge, wall-to-wall projections of images in which the subject could be in a cab simulator watching so much visual input that is projected around him to include the periphery that he feels he is in the simulation.

Augmented reality displays are displays, typically pilots can look through and see the real world augmented with images hanging in thin air, such as targeting or radar readouts. Telepresence reality systems have been used in surgical applications to see 3D images inside the patient. At the top of the hierarchy is the immersion systems in which a user dons a head-mounted display which senses movements of the head to redraw the visual images with each movement. The higher the number of pixels the more realistic the picture seems to the eye. Resolution near 1280 pixels by 1024 will produce pictures that approach movie quality. Polygons are the geometric mesh that texels are put in to create the texture of an object. Sound is a relatively inexpensive enhancement to virtual reality systems that derive the most depth without increasing the visual display.

When systems are embellished with rich sounds, such as race car simulations where the user can hear the engine of the approaching car, hear it go by, then hear the roaring of the crowd as he passes, the picture can be just better than marginal yet the experience will be greater due to the richness of the sensory stimulation. Tactile sensors such as gloves are often associated with virtual reality systems. But for the purposes of academic applications, such expense is not warranted. Instead, a simple navigation device, such as a pointer or two pointers, would bring about the ability to open, close, start events, grasp and pour items, just as well as expensive haptic devices. Home virtual reality systems are the same as the academic models, built for fewer users.

Virtual reality is the medium that could transform a classroom into any environment appropriate to the task, due to its very nature of created world architecture. Exploration and uncovering in the virtual environment is not limited to the realm of the possible. The best part of education is learning from mistakes. In the virtual environment, mistakes are not harmful and experiences can be repeated.

Teachers must appreciate the fact that virtual environments teach content and processes in the same theme. While the current flight simulation technology used with professional airline pilots does not teach one to fly, it is used to ensure the integration of new sequences, thus new patterns and situations are understood. In this manner, educators could place the virtual reality simulations either in the beginning of the lecture to build on current vocabulary skills, or with sequential data to understand dynamic functions and relational information to take back to the classroom where the teacher could begin to manipulate what was learned in the virtual environment.

Virtual reality uses sight and sound to create the environment while allowing the user to navigate "inside" an environment much the way we do naturally with much greater recall than simply reading or passively watching. Today pilots are required to recall thousands of sequences leading to hundreds of events without being permitted any mistakes in real-life execution of those duties. In this setting, the cost is not an issue. For military training missions, this is not the case. In the light of tremendous budget cuts, the level of readiness must be high while keeping the cost to a minimum.

Training transfer has not been quantified by the military nor the airline industry due to the extreme cost of the simulators coupled with the almost constant use of the machines. The costs of these systems are near astronomical in terms of education software and hardware systems. Using virtual reality as a delivery system for this approach is the idea behind the video games which have most children transfixed by the hour. The user is "inside" the environment, exploring the many items, manipulating them, and coming up with ideas to get to the reward. This tension built into the video game, coupled with a journey, is the most motivating aspect of gaming.

In the Electronic Entertainment Exposition in Los Angeles, CA, hundreds of video games were reviewed by users and were rated by how many were purchased as well as how well the games performed. Thousands of users responded electronically and in person as well as by other means. Those with the richest pictures and most realistic motions were the favourites. Those with the most to gain from winning were highly prized and those with the better sound effects were favoured above all the other types tried. This is no surprise to educators. Psychologists for flight simulators agree that pilots remember the richer experiences, enhanced with sound, motion, and self-directed navigation through the environment. In addition to the need of educators to present the information in a personal situation to the student, the experience is enhanced when it can be shared with others. The shared experience tends to engage new ideas and questions brought about by collaborative investigation.

The military has used this paradigm in the SIMNET system for years, where several individuals are immersed in the same battlefield scene, each with a mission. The interaction is not only with the simulation, but with each other as well. The outcome is a richer experience than being there alone. The game DOOM does the same thing for its users. There, the situation is a space station where the user is in a "kill or be killed" situation. Virtual reality delivery systems can be created to represent any situation desired. Preteaching can occur in the classroom in preparation for the virtual experience. The value of this experience was learning that the preteaching had a large impact on the outcome of the experience.

Virtual reality can be used for preteaching the field trip or for remediation. Teachers are also looking for delivery systems that illustrate basic attributes, examples and non-examples, relational identities, classification theory, definition, summation and so on. Observation is the first thing the student does, then he classifies the observations into groups, etc. The game industry has integrated all these attributes, and students learn what is required to win the game and live to fight another day.

A system should be designed in the basic research and development model:

i) Build a team to manage the project to include teachers, technical consultant, and a programmer.
ii) Chart the intended outcomes to include wishes and desires of teachers and users.
iii) Develop training transfer evaluation model.

Get the requirements from the teachers who will be the recipients of the student users. Include a focus group of student users early in the design of the system.

A typical system set up in each school library assures that the appropriate personnel would maintain the system. The librarian would schedule class rotation to maximise usage of the system according to the needs of the teachers. This would allow teachers to use the tool before their lecture or after it, at their discretion. The home unit is simply a standard desktop computer with a head-mounted display attached. Schedules of multiple user programming could be downloaded periodically to ensure maximum participation of the home scholar or distance learner with interaction with a school activity. Before attempting to create any new courseware, play many games to understand where to place graphic user interfaces naturally in the virtual environment. The games that do the best job of holding the attention of the user are equipped with a guide. Keep user's orientation relative to the ground as natural as possible. This will decrease the likelihood of becoming disoriented. Persons with disabilities can benefit from virtual reality delivery systems because their physical condition is not a limitation in the synthetic experience.

Variables in these systems are the number of processor/ headset systems needed, the amount of software development required, and the level of sophistication necessary to deliver the quality of virtual environment desired. The first components researched were the head-mounted displays. There is quite a shakedown of this manufacturing segment at the moment. Many have gone out of business this year alone. Virtual Reality Incorporated is committed to providing wholesale to the education market. The product line is mid-range and more than adequate for home or classroom use. Forte Technologies has a headset that is comparable at the same price. They are entering the education market with a new product that is less bulky than the conventional headset which allows the choice of immersion or not. The hardware needed to run school systems is extremely complex and needs to be developed school by school to ensure that the needs of that facility are met. Software, on the other hand, may be created almost generically as is done with textbooks. In fact, it is an extremely good idea to make as many recyclable parts of the curriculum to cut down creation times. Software houses use this technique and Sonalyst is excellent at doing so.

When designing software, in accordance with the wishes of the educator, it may be desirable to build in an editor that allows the student to create their own documentaries to be the repository of what they have learned. Educators have very special needs and are the providers of the tax payers of tomorrow and deserve the very best virtual reality systems offered. As such, the systems that are designed must be: (a) in line with legacy systems of today and (b) must be so far reaching as not to be obsolete by the time they arrive at the school and the boxes are opened. The most important recommendation that can be made to the educator is to get a development consultant early in the process. The consultant will save the school time and money from the first day.

Without a consultant, teachers will have to evaluate head-mounted displays, learn how to programme for the virtual reality simulation, decide which software packages are best for which hardware platforms and what is the latest and greatest configurations and so on. It is also financially dangerous to buy a system from a vendor that only sells one brand. The situation is akin to buying insurance from a provider that carries only one line. He can offer you only one brand. A development consultant will search for the provider that has what you, the individual educator, desires. Periodically, test the system for outdated content. Maintenance on the virtual reality delivery system is the same for any computer system. A simulation should be a journey as specified earlier with many processes included. Paradigm Simulations does an excellent job in providing high end, high resolution software applications.

Many teachers have been obliged to catch up with children in the skills of using calculators and computers, and to struggle with how they should best be used in education, long after they had become commonplace in classrooms. Teacher educators have an opportunity now to learn from these experiences, and ensure that initial and in-service courses begin to prepare teachers to use virtual reality effectively, and to deal with issues that will inevitably arise from this new medium. The opportunity to avoid having to play catch-up will not, however, last for long.

There have been specific proposals for ways of using VR, including: visiting inaccessible places or historical scenes; manipulating simulations of the real world, without the danger, expense or time consumption of doing the real thing; exploring places and things more effectively because of alterations in scale and time; learning algebra in a virtual world where the behaviour of objects demonstrates the axioms of algebra. Underlying such proposals for using VR in schools are a number of assumptions about potential educational benefits which are either unique to VR, or less evident in other media.

Three assumptions in particular are prominent, and they focus on VR's positive impacts on spatial thinking, interest level and individual learning. If these assumptions are warranted, VR will be a powerful tool which deserves prominent coverage in teacher training.

The impact of VR on the aspect of spatial thinking is important, because children need to be able to generalise classroom knowledge to the outside world. The result is, nevertheless, intriguing because it would seem reasonable to assume a fundamental link between visualising shapes from various viewpoints and recognising shapes, or parts of them, in everyday objects. Any such link was not revealed by asking children to draw shapes, even though generous allowance was made during scoring for lack of drawing skill. This finding carries a fundamental message for teacher training. No matter how compelling a logical link might appear, it is essential to put assumptions about how children learn to the test.

It is not clear what particular characteristics of VR contributed to the skill of recognising shapes in everyday objects that was not available to the control group children who worked with card models. The VR group worked much more enthusiastically than the control group, but lack of impact by VR on some tasks suggests that the gains made were not attributable solely to motivation or novelty.

In a study of upper primary children, Ainge compared recall of details in a virtual scene with recall of details from a series of photographs of the scene. The scene was a single furnished room which the children explored at will. On the one hand, the intuitive expectation that a sense of actually being in the virtual room would enhance recall of all details better than photographs was not supported. The children remembered which objects were in the room, and their colours, just as well from studying the photographs. Although the children were new to VR, were enthusiastic, and made comments about enjoying it, their enjoyment did not lead to better recall across the board. On the other hand VR had a significantly stronger impact than the photographs on children's recollection of numbers of each object and location of objects relative to each other. There was no indication as to how VR enhanced recall of numbers of objects. The photographs consisted of multiple views of the room, and showed the objects just as clearly as the virtual scene. Some children did, however, make comments while studying the photographs which indicated how VR may have helped them to remember positions of objects.

Although the verbal instructions made clear that the 18 photographs were all of a single room, some children revealed that they were visualising more than one room. This did not occur with the virtual room. In VR it was possible to see at a glance that there was only one room, but some children clearly had difficulty in synthesising the photographs into a whole. These findings strongly suggest that aspects of teacher training which deal with the development of children's spatial thinking, in particular, but not limited to, mathematics, should inform teachers about the significant contribution which VR can make.

VR does not entertain in the way that a film or video does. The display of a virtual scene remains static until the user makes things happen, by exploration or manipulating objects. The novelty of the technology appealed to the children and they were anxious to become involved. More significantly, however, it was found that interest remained high even after several experiences, without any sign of reduction. Pantelidis led a group that produced virtual reconstructions of a native North American Indian fort, using 'virtues walk-through'. Middle School children were given a lesson about the fort, then explored the reconstructions. Pantelidis reports that the children were very enthusiastic and wanted to find out how the Indians had lived.

In the study of VR's impact on learning about three dimensional shapes, Ainge found that the children, who normally tended to participate reluctantly in classroom activities, maintained their enthusiasm over a period of six weeks. Throughout the work with VR, not one student required any encouragement to remain on task, and many were reluctant to stop when their session came to an end. The teacher was impressed by the high level of student engagement and enthusiasm, which contrasted sharply with the response to other classroom activities. Each student was interviewed at the completion of the study, and responses indicated a unanimous feeling that VR had helped them learn, a high level of enjoyment of VR, and strong maintenance of interest. Fifteen children reported after six weeks that VR was at least as enjoyable as when they first began and seventeen said that they preferred learning with VR rather than other activities. Given teachers' widespread concerns about difficulty in motivating children to participate effectively in classroom activities, it is imperative that teachers be made aware of VR's strong potential for engaging pupils. Given that there is only limited understanding at this stage of VR's educational potential, teachers in training should be encouraged to join the research effort and seek to identify a range of activities which could be made more enjoyable by the use of VR.

When children actively pursue their individual strategies for exploring virtual scenes, they should learn better than when they take a passive role in the classroom. They anticipate that learning will combine cognitive, affective, and psychomotor skills as children pursue their own learning strategies. Apart from finding that after the VR practice the children were significantly faster and more accurate in real world shopping, they investigated change in self-directed activity. They found that over the period of the VR sessions there was a significant decrease in teacher input, and in particular, instruction and physical guidance decreased at a faster rate than more open ended assistance. Some children moved about slowly, as if they were cautious, and sometimes were startled by movements. The boys tended to make more rapid movements than the girls, although this did not apply in all cases. Some children referred to flying and enjoyed zooming in on shapes at high speed.

A virtual hand was available, controlled by the mouse, and it could be made to grasp shapes and move them around or rotate them. Some children used the hand whereas others practically ignored it. Some children took the option of switching it off. At times, all children made movements which resulted in their shapes disappearing from view. The way that children addressed this problem revealed a range of approaches from impulsive to thoughtful. Some children gave a running commentary on what was happening, others said very little. When the children were asked about their work with VR, their responses indicated that they had interacted with VR in individual ways. They each had their own views on how VR had helped them learn, ways it could be improved, and what they liked most and least, about it. The view that learners not only should, but inevitably do, construct their learning, rather than simply acquire information, is widely accepted.

VR SYSTEMS

Researches on multi-user virtual environments can be classified into two categories:

- — network-based VR systems, and
- — web-based VR systems.

The first category of the multiple user virtual reality system does not necessarily comply with the architecture of the web environment. This type of virtual reality system generally focuses on providing a large-scale multiple user virtual environment with every available network technique. The web-based multiple user virtual reality system emphasises providing collaborative virtual environments on top of the existent web environment.

Network-based multi-user systems: When a multi-user virtual environment over the internet is built the important problems should be taken to consideration are:

i) the spatial consistency problem and

ii) the time coherency problem.

Due to the intrinsic network latency, time coherency is almost an insolvable problem for the researchers. Hence, most of the researches of the networked virtual environment have focused on the spatial consistency problem. Various methods have been proposed to maintain the consistency of the synthetic world among distributed players. These methods include communication protocols to log in an existent virtual world and to share the status of objects among distributed participants. These communication protocols are tightly related to the database models used by the networked virtual reality systems.

According to the distribution of the virtual world database, the networked virtual environments are four categories:

i) *Replicated homogeneous world database:* The two delegations of the replicated homogeneous world model are SIMNET and NPSNET. The NPSNET system uses the Distributive Interactive Simulation (DIS) standard, which is descended from the SIMNET, to communicate the entity status changes among distributed players.

ii) *Shared and centralised database:* The systems that employ shared and centralised database model are RING and VLNET. VLNET focuses on providing realistic virtual human characters inside the virtual world. To achieve such a goal, different protocols were designed for the object behaviour, navigation, body posture etc.

iii) *Shared and distributed database with peer-to-peer updates:* DIVE system has fully duplicated homogeneous and distributed databases. However, the entire databases are dynamic and a reliable multicast protocol is used to actively replicate new objects.

iv) *Shared, distributed and client-server databases*: To scale up the number of participants without compensating the shared object consistency, BRICKNET and MASSIVE systems employ shared, distributed and client-server databases to achieve the goal. BRICKNET took one step further to allow objects' dynamic behaviours to be shared among distributed players. MASSIVE uses a spatial model for database partition among clients.

With the emergence of the VRML standard that brings the virtual world into the web environment, researches on supporting the multi-user interaction on the web environment have become a popular topic.

Web-based multi-user systems: In the traditional web architecture, due to the intrinsic nature of HTTP used, it is impossible to achieve the interactivity among users. Hence mechanisms and protocols have to be designed to support the multiple user interactions on the web environment. Several researches on the web-based collaborative systems have their own proprietary methods to support the multiple user interaction.

The most famous web-based multi-user system is the Virtual Society (VS). It is a research project of Sony Computer Science Laboratory. The project is an attempt to define a global architecture and a set of protocols to realise a multi-user interactive 3D environment in a WWW setting. Large-scale shared 3D spaces using the VRML, the Virtual Society proposed a so-called Virtual Society Server Client Protocol (VSCP) to extend the function of the existing VRML standard. A scripting architecture is also designed for different levels of consistency for the shared objects. However, the Virtual Society architecture is not seaMLless integrated with the web environment. The VS server is an independent programme from the WWW server. Consequently, the Virtual Society does not support information exchange between the data on an HTML document and the objects inside a virtual world. Hence, the Virtual Society is an extension of the networked virtual reality system to the web environment rather than merges the networked virtual reality system into the web architecture.

Another type of web-based multi-user system proposed by German National Research Centre for Information Technology does not require a multi-user server to maintain the consistency among distributed objects. Instead, after a VRML scene file has been downloaded from a web server, the browser introduces itself as a user to the server. The web server responds to this new user with an embodiment file of all existing players, along with a multicast address and a port number. The multicast address refers to the IP address of the web server, and the port number denotes an existing virtual world. Hence, during the course of interaction, each participant sends its status change to the specified port on the web server and listens to the update information of other users from another port representing a multicast channel. Since each individual client sends the update messages to the specified port and the web server redistributes the messages through a multicast channel, an extended HTTPD server is designed to receive update information to monitor the status of the virtual world.

Another approach to integrate the multi-user virtual environment with the web is the Scalable Platform for Large Interactive Networked Environment (SPLINE) came from Mitsubishi Electric Research Lab (MERL). Spline is essentially a network-based multi-user virtual reality system that uses Interactive Sharing Transfer Protocol (ISTP) as its communication protocol. ISTP incorporated several simple HTTP protocols to enable the HTTP server to participate the multi-user interaction.

Other famous web-based multi-user systems which are commercially available are OnLive! Technologies Inc., OZ Virtual, Ccpro and V*Realm Multi-User. All of these browsers adapt the VRML standard as their virtual scene file format, and each system uses its proprietary technique to provide interactivity among distributed users.

The only standardised communication protocol for multi-user interaction over the internet is the DIS standard. The DIS standard is originally designed for peer-to-peer simulation and aims at military training simulation, however, its concept has been adapted by other distributed virtual reality systems.

The DIS standard links the interactive, free play activities of people in an operational exercise to form a time and space coherent synthetic world. This synthetic environment is created through the low latency exchange of data units between distributed, computationally autonomous simulation applications. These computational simulation applications may be presented in one location or distributed geographically. Two important techniques have been defined in the DIS standard. They are:

i) Protocol Data Unit (PDU) model, and
ii) Dead Reckoning (DR) model.

The PDU is the data unit that defines the information exchanged among simulation hosts through the network. The PDU contains the information of simulated entity status and the type of interaction that took place in an operational, exercise. It also defines the data format for the simulation management to monitor the simulation process. The DIS defines 27 types of PDUs, which are organised into six protocol families. They are:

i) entity information/interaction,
ii) warfare,
iii) logistics,
iv) simulation management,
v) distributed emission regeneration,
vi) radio communication.

The purpose of the DIS technique is to link the simulated entities distributed over geographically separated sites. The Dead Reckon model is used to estimate each entity's position and orientation based upon the pervious information. The objective of Dead Reckon model is to reduce traffic load on the network when maintaining the spatial consistency among simulated entities.

For each simulated entity, the Dead Reckoning model uses its previous updated information to predict its next position and orientation called Dead Reckon values. A host uses the Dead Reckon values to move distributive simulated entities before their actual postures are received from the network. For the simulated entity that is controlled by a host, its Dead Reckon value is calculated along with its actual position and orientation.

With the Dead Reckoning technique, it is not necessary for a host to send an Entity State PDU of a simulated entity about every change in position and orientation that occurs over the time. Only when the Dead Reckon value of an entity is different from its actual posture by a predetermined threshold, a new Entity State PDU for that entity is actually sent onto the network.

3D Web Browsing System

The 3D web browsing systems have became unavoidable parts of the virtual world. Here we are the describing the SharedWeb system. It is a collaborative 3D web browsing system designed in Multimedia and Virtual Reality Lab, Tamkang University. The goal of the SharedWeb system is to support interaction among clients over the existing web environment. By the seaMLess integration of the network-based virtual reality system with the web architecture, the SharedWeb system provides a boundless way to retrieve information over the web environment while the users are interacting with each other.

The existent web server uses the request-and-response technique for its clients to retrieve information, because of the distinct characteristics of the HTTP protocol. Thus, the link between the server and the client is established only when a client issues a request to the server. This link is broken and "forgotten" immediately by the server after the requested information is sent to that client.

The web architecture imposes four intrinsic problems on the support of the multiple user interactions. They are:

i) *Client information records:* Because the link is broken immediately after the server has sent the requested information to the client, the server generally does not keep the records of the clients who have requested information from it. This is called the client information recording problem. This problem can slove, each browser must be able to provide a sequence number, called Unique Identification (UID), to uniquely identify itself to the server. The SharedWeb browser uses the combination of LTP, which stands for Login name, Time stamp and listen Port number. The login name is the nickname of the user who logins to a virtual world. Whereas, the Time stamp is the time when the browser is first activated and the listen port number is the port number that the browser uses to receive messages. With is UID number, the SharedWeb server can easily identify a new registed player and assign a user ID to that browser.

ii) *Server-to-client callback:* Because the HTTP link between the server and the client is establish only when a specific request is raised by a client, the web server does not have any information to actively set up a connection to its client. Therefore, if a client intends to send information to other clients in the same virtual world, the server does not have the ability to forward this information to those clients. This is referred as the Server-to-client callback problem. This problem can solve, the server has to remember the browsers that were registered to a virtual scene. Each browser must also provide its information, such as IP address and port number to the server, so that the server can actively send information to the registered browser. With the Client Information Recording method, the SharedWeb browser sends the UID information to the SharedWeb server after a user has logged in. When the SharedWeb server receives the registration information from a browser, it saves this registration message and replies the registered browser with its IP address and port number. Therefore, during the course of the multi-user interaction, each registered browser sends its status change to the SharedWeb server and the SharedWeb server then actively forwards the received message.

The cookie technique is another widely used one. It is based on a two-stage process. First, a "cookie", or a small piece of information, is sent by the web server and stored in the user's computer without its consent or knowledge. Second the cookie clandestinely and automatically establishes connection to the web server.

iii) *Excessive network loading:* Although a web-based multi-user virtual reality system does not necessarily require a multi-user server to maintain the spatial consistency of a virtual world, still, a central server is required to mediate communication among the clients. The network bandwidth will be overloaded very quickly, as the number of players increases, and the server will rapidly become an input/output bottleneck as well. This situation is described as an Excessive Network Loading problem. Since the DIS standard is a fully distributed simulation method, the DIS concept is adapted by the SharedWeb system to reduce this problem. Each SharedWeb browser has the entire virtual world information. The status change information of an entity is also encapsulated into a self-contained data package, called protocol data unit (PDU), which is forwarded to each participating browser through the SharedWeb server. With the PDU, the frequency of data transmission is reduced. With the help of the Dead Reckoning model from the DIS standard, the status change information needs not to be transmitted so often. As guided by the Dead Reckoning model, the status change of an entity is sent to the server when this change exceeds a predefined threshold. Hence, the bandwidth requirement is further reduced.

iv) *Virtual world entrance:* The web server must be able to send the IP address and the port number of a multi-user server to its clients. Commonly the web architecture employs the request-and-response method of HTTP, so that the web server is not aware of the client who has downloaded a scene file. The web server cannot automatically forward the information of the multi-user server to that client. The problem is referred as virtual world entrance. To solve this problem, we can either embed the multi-user server information into the downloaded scene file or allow the client to issue a query message to the WWW server for the information of the multi-user server. The first option is simpler, but it will cause trouble when a multi-user server is crashed and a replacement server is activated. As to the second option, the client has to wait until the replied HTML document is received before it then can connect to the virtual world.

In the web architecture, the web server uses the Common Gateway Interface (CGI) programme to communicate with its add on application. Hence, a CGI programme can be used to forward the login information from the web server to the multi-user server, and, thus, the client does not care if the multi-user server and the web server reside in the same host. A hierarchy structure of the multi-user servers can be implemented so that the web server can pass client login information to a load-monitor programme, which can forward the client transparently to another multi-user server.

The SharedWeb system provides a natural extension of the web environment into a multi-user virtual environment. The nodes of the SharedWeb system can be classified into two types: the server site and the browser site. The browser site is composed of four modules:

i) Multiple participants interface,
ii) 3D render engine,
iv) Chat phase,
v) WWW Homepage Viewer modules.

The server site is designed as an add-on application of the existing web server with two modules: a CGI programme and the Sharedweb server. The server and the browser communicate through the SharedWeb Communication Protocol (SWCP).

Multiple participant interface module runs on top of Winsock to manipulate the interaction between the browser and other players. This module is the kernel of a SharedWeb browser. Its main functions are to calculate browser's UID, encapsulate and de-capsulate the PDUs, transmit/receive data to/from the network, and coordinate messages among 3D Render Engine, Chat Phase, and WWW Homepage Viewer modules. The 3D Render Engine module provides a visual window for the user to explore the virtual world. When a browser retrieves a scene file from the web server, it is an ASCII file. The scene file is then translated into a virtual world database recognised by the 3D Render Engine module. The Chat Phase module is designed to support text communication among distributed players. This module enhances the interactions among distributed participants and, hence, broadens the applicability of the SharedWeb system. The shared virtual world will be a wordless world that makes the user bored easily when playing with the SharedWeb browser. The WWW Homepage Viewer module is a standard HTML browser. By seaMLessly integrating this module into the SharedWeb browser, a user can enter another virtual world by double clicking a hyperlink provided on a homepage or inside the virtual world.

The server site is a gateway for a SharedWeb user to enter a virtual world. A user only needs to download a scene file from this web server and logs in a nickname to enter a virtual world. After the web server receives the login information from a browser, it passes the received user information to the SharedWeb server through the CGI programme. The SharedWeb server module is the kernel of the entire SharedWeb system. This programme is responsible for mediating the information exchange among the browsers in the same virtual world.

The communication protocol includes steps to join an existent virtual world, to forward messages among distributed users, and to leave the virtual world. On the other hand, the DIS standard is so far the most successful technique that enables a fully distributed virtual environment to be built on the internet. The DIS standard, even though it was not designed for the web, has been proven to effectively support the networked multi-user virtual environment on the internet. The extensions focus on the methods to fully integrate the networked virtual reality system into the existing web architecture.

There are seven PDUs defined for the SharedWeb system. Most of them are composed of two common portions and other related fields.

The first common portion is called PDU Header. Since the SharedWeb system supports more than one scenario at a time, each PDU contains a PDU Header to identify a user in different scenes. The PDU header is composed of the following fields:

i) Protocol Version,
ii) PDU Type,
iii) Time Stamp,
iv) Scene Name,
v) Scene ID.

The Protocol Version field is used to identify the SWCP version. The PDU Type field tells the receiver what kind of PDU it is, such as Initial PDU, Object State PDU, End PDU, Acknowledge PDU, Chat PDU, HTTP PDU, or Error PDU. The Time Stamp field records the time when this PDU was sent and it can be used to justify the validation of the user's message. The Scene Name stores the file name of the downloaded virtual scene, and the Scene ID is the unique identification number of the downloaded virtual scene. The SharedWeb server uses the Scene Name and Scene ID fields to recognise the virtual world in which the browser issuing the PDU resides.

The second common portion for most PDUs is the User Information. It contains the information for a user to identify himself/herself, and is comprised by the following fields:

i) User ID,
ii) IP address,
iii) Avatar type.

The User ID stores the identification number of a browser inside a virtual world, and it is assigned by the SharedWeb server when the user logs in to a virtual world. The Avatar Type field gives the user an option to choose his/her represented shape inside the virtual world.

To control the process of a SharedWeb browser to enter a virtual world, the SharedWeb uses two PDUs, the Initial PDU and the Acknowledge PDU, Similarly, the End PDU and the Acknowledge PDU are used to communicate the event of a SharedWeb browser leaving a virtual world. In addition to the PDU Header and the User Information portions, these three PDUs have another important portion called UID. This UID is calculated by the browser when the browser is activated. The SharedWeb server saves this UID number in its client table, and uses this information to communicate with that specific browser. Unlike the User ID field of the User Information, which is unique within a virtual world only, the UID uniquely identifies a user from others at all times even if they do not reside in the same virtual world.

The UID field contains the following three fields:

i) Login User Name,
ii) Time,
iii) Port number.

The Initial PDU allows a browser to submit the information to the SharedWeb server to log into a virtual world. After a browser has downloaded a scene file from a web server, an Initial PDU is created when the user keys in a login nickname. However, the SharedWeb browser is not aware of the existence of the SharedWeb server when it downloads a scene file from a web server. The Sharedweb browser sends the Initial PDU as an HTTP string directly to the web server. When the web server receives this HTTP string, it activates a CGI programme to forward this Initial PDU to the SharedWeb server.

Using this methodology, the SharedWeb server acts as an add-on function to the existing web server. Another benefit of this method is the possibility of providing the load balance and the fault tolerance features on the multi-user server site. Since the CGI programme is used to mediate the login process, the web server can easily transfer a new login-user to a different SharedWeb server if the previous server is overloaded or crashed. When the SharedWeb server receives the Initial PDU from a browser, it responds with an Acknowledge PDU to the browser. This Acknowledge PDU has the same fields and contents as the Initial PDU except the PDU Type and Time Stamp. This Acknowledge PDU is used by the SharedWeb server to verify that an Initial PDU has been received and to send the assigned unique User ID back to the browser. When a user wants to exit a virtual world, the browser sends an End PDU to notify the SharedWeb server. The End PDU contains the same data format, except the PDU Type and Time Stamp, as the Initial PDU.

When the SharedWeb server receives the End PDU, it first removes the corresponding avatar information from its client table and responds to this event by issuing an Acknowledge PDU to that browser. The SharedWeb sever also forwards the End PDU to other browsers so that they can remove its represented avatars from their respective virtual world.

For the DIS protocol, the Entity State PDU is the most important PDU because it is used to exchange the status information among the distributed entities. Similarly, the SWCP defines an Object State PDU to mirror the Entity State PDU. However, from the perspective of the SharedWeb system design goal, the definition of the Object State PDU is not as complicated as that of the Entity State PDU. In addition to the PDU Header and User Information, the object State PDU contains the following fields:

i) Location,

ii) Linear Velocity,

iii) Orientation,

iv) DR Parameter.

Location, Linear Velocity and Orientation fields define the postures of an avatar, which represents the user inside a virtual world. The DR Parameter field is set by the browser to specify the parameter for the Dead Reckoning model that controls the movement of an avatar. After successfully logging in to the virtual world, the browser uses the Object State PDU to send the status information of an avatar to the SharedWeb server. Based upon the Dead Reckoning model being used, the Object State PDU is issued only when the actual position of its represented avatar exceeds its Dead Reckon value by a predefined threshold.

Chatting is an important feature to enhance collaboration among the distributed users. The SharedWeb system adopts a widely accepted chatting protocol called the Internet Relay Protocol (IRP) to design the Chat PDU. Since the IRP is a peer-to-peer chatting protocol, Chat PDU is the only PDU that bypasses the SharedWeb server. The Chat PDU includes the PDU Header portion for the receiver to verify that the sender is within the same virtual world and two additional fields: Sender ID and Text Massage. Although a chat server can be designed to support group chatting, it can generate a bottleneck on the SharedWeb server site as the number of players increases.

Design goal of the SharedWeb system is not only to provide a seaMLess way to support multiple user interactions on the web environment, but also to furnish a method to integrate the web resources. An HTTP PDU is implemented to achieve this goal. The HTTP PDU allows the user to send a URL address of a web resource, such as an HTML document or sound, to other users. After a browser receives an HTTP PDU, it downloads the specific web resource from the specified URL location. Particularly, the HTTP PDU enables the user to control the objects in the virtual world from an HTML document. Whenever the forms of an HTML document on the SharedWeb browser are filled and sent, these data are sent to the web server.

The web server forwards the received information to the SharedWeb server through the CGI programme. Hence, In addition PDU Header, the HTTP PDU has the following format:

i) Receiver ID,
ii) URL Address,
iii) Events field.

Receiver ID field contains the User ID that is going to receive this PDU. URL Address field is the network location of the specified web resource, and Events field is a string of data that were filled in the forms of the HTML document. With this particular PDU, a user can easily send his/her HTML document or other resource to the other users in the same virtual world.

The SharedWeb server is run on Windows NT Server ver 4.0 with an embedded WWW server. For the sake of flexibility and extendibility, the SharedWeb browser was implemented as a standalone browser at this moment. The SharedWeb browser will be implemented as a plug-in application for the Netscape Communicator or the internet Explorer in the near future.

There are four factors which are affecting the interaction among the distributed users.

i) The bandwidth required by the SharedWeb browser to reflect the status change of an avatar;
ii) The network latency between the SharedWeb server and browser,
iii) The network bandwidth provided by the network structure, such as the internet;
iv) The computational load or the SharedWeb server in forwarding the received PDUs;

The first factor depends upon the size of the Object State PDU and how often this PDU is sent by the SharedWeb browser. By multiplying the size of the Object State PDU by the number of the PDU that is sent by a browser per second, the bandwidth required by a single user can be easily decided. Significantly, this factor will decide not only the network bandwidth required for the SharedWeb system but also the number of players that can be interacting simultaneously. The second and third factors completely depend upon the network structure, such as a local area network or a wide area network that is used. With the help of the Dead Reckoning model, the second and third factors have little influence on the interaction among the distributed users. The fourth factor is a constant time since the SharedWeb server simply records and forwards the received PDUs according to the information saved on its Client Table.

With the Dead Reckoning model the number of the Object State PDUs sent to the network is minimised. The equation of Dead Reckoning model used by the SharedWeb system is a linear equation, $P = P_0 + V^*t$. In this equation, P stands for Dead Reckon (DR) value and P_0 is the last updated actual position. The velocity *V* is the speed of movement of an avatar. The most important factor of this equation is the definition of the time *t*. Instead of using the host clock, *r* is defined as the logical time of the virtual world. This definition will ensure that the movement of avatars will not be affected by the computational power of each host, and the computation of the Dead Reckoning model is simplified consequently.

Different virtual worlds were constructed to explore the features of the SharedWeb system fully. The include virtual campus, virtual office 3D wargaming environment etc..

The virtual campus application aimed to investigate the possibility of designing a virtual university over the web environment. It provides a new way for to students to visit the campus without leaving their desks. Inside the virtual campus, the students can chat with each other while navigating the virtual campus. Each building inside this virtual campus has a hyperlink to another virtual world that models the interior of that building. If a building has many storeys, it will contain hyperlinks to more than one virtual world and each floor is modelled as a virtual world.

The virtual office application is an effort to study the possibility of performing some of the university's administrative tasks online. Since the SharedWeb system is an integration of the virtual reality system with the HTML browser, a user can use the HTML document to fill the application form, say, for a new student ID. Various application forms are hyperlinked by pictures on the wall inside this virtual office. The user can click one of the pictures to download an application form to the HTML browser. Since the application form is implemented as an HTML document, different types of the application form can be easily designed and modified.

The 3D wargaming simulation application is a 3D version of a Role Playing Game (RPG) simulation, where the player can choose his role-inside the game. The character of the game is controlled by the user's command rather than being directly manipulated by the input device, such as joysticks. The RPG is traditionally using a two-dimension graphical layout. In addition, it requires an interactive dialogue box, or command sheet, for the player to control his character inside the game. Since the SharedWeb system fully integrates the HTML browser with the virtual reality navigator, the command sheet can be easily implemented by an HTML document. In addition a game master, which is required for an RPG to control the game rules, was implemented in the SharedWeb server. This prototype 3D wargaming system allows three users to enter a virtual battlefield. One user plays the blue tank commander by logging in as "bluetank", another plays the red tank commander by typing in "redtank" as his user name, and the third player is the referee of this combat exercise. Blue tank and red tank commanders can use forms and check boxes that are available on the HTML document to control two tanks inside the virtual battlefield.

VIRTUAL EDUCATIONAL INSTITUTIONS

Human resources are the most valuable resources of any nation. The conventional methods of teaching and educating engineers and technicians cannot cope with the scale and magnitude of the urgent need, because of the high-tech revolution. A number of new initiatives have been taken recently with the main objective of making engineering education not only cost-effective but also accessible to a large number of people. These new initiatives are based on satellite delivery of courses from one location to another locations simultaneously. The magnitude of increase in industrial human resources required in the engineering workforce cannot be achieved by conventional educational system for many reasons.

Conventional classroom teaching methods are based on a staff-student ratio of normally 1 to 10. A substantial increase in intake into technical education institutions would mean substantial increase in the faculty strength. Even if it is possible to train faculty in sufficient numbers, most of these faculty members will be inexperienced for a long time to come. Students would not have the benefits of teaching by experienced and expert academics. There is a need for a well-stocked on-campus library facilities. Libraries in most developing countries have collection of obsolete materials. Lack of sufficient funds hinders acquisition of up-to-date books and journals.

Another problem is with the retraining and skills upgrading of existing technical manpower. To keep up with the rapidly changing global environment retraining and education have to be lifelong. Lifelong education is not possible as it will take engineers away from their workplaces every time. Engineers of today are to be global in skills, attitudes, and ability to be able to participate productively in the current environment of globalisation of economy and the information technology revolution. Internationally marketable skills, global thinking, and the ability to respond to the rapidly changing global environment can be imparted only by a curriculum that has a global character and by programmes which have inputs not just from a team of local experts but from a team consisting of best experts from around the country. A number of initiatives taken very recently are good examples of the alternative approaches to technical education.

The National Technological University (NTU) was established in Colorado, US, as a non-profit corporation in January 1984. NTU was the first institution to use satellite-based delivery of instructions on an expansive scale. It offers a wide range of ITV courses through satellites to a large number of sites in the US and the Pacific Rim Countries. The course are taught by top faculty from 47 participating leading engineering schools in the country. Starting with 33 courses from 13 participating universities in 1984 the NTU programmes have grown into more than 1,300 courses from 47 participating universities. In 1995-96 NTU offered through satellite broadcasting more than 22,000 hours of credit instructions and 3,000 hours non-credit advanced technology and management programmes.

The African Virtual University (AVU) project grew out of the desperate need for mass tertiary education in science and technology in Africa. The UNESCO is promoting the concept of satellite-based universities in science and technology in four regions of the world—the Arab States, Eastern Europe-Central Asia, Latin America and Africa. The programme proposes, among other functions, to technological and scientific human resources base in Africa, if the continent is to participate in the global economy and seize the opportunities created by globalisation of economies and information technology revolution. The AVU will be unique in the role it will play in the economic and social transformation of Africa through mass tertiary education in science, technology and management. While NTU brings the education and technology to the doors of the professionals who need training and education, the technology is already available within the country.

UNESCO is promoting the concept of satellite-based universities in science and technology in the Arab States, Eastern Europe-Central-Asia Latin America and Africa. The programme proposes among other functions to:

i) Develop a core group of universities in the region committed to developing and offering programmes in science and technology via satellite throughout the region;
ii) Select a few of the core group as initial uplink centres for delivering procured scientific and technological education material; and
iii) Establish international links with leading universities in the US and Europe for sharing knowledge.

Some of the end objectives of the programme are:

i) Increasing the skills and capabilities of scientists, technocrats, professionals, and managers by providing them opportunities for professional development in their workplace through ITV via satellite;

ii) Supporting present national and regional network of open universities; and

iii) Increasing public awareness on the importance of science and technology.

Today, education is undergoing a revolution. For-profit institutions are expanding at a great rate and old ideas about profit and non-profit are being challenged. Today, the fastest growing university in the US is a for-profit organisation. The university which supports its research/educational and administrative activities which leap over the boundaries of time and space can be termed as a virtual university. The idea of virtual university concepts include distance learning and virtual classes. This ideal educational development of virtual university is created by the support of infra information systems. To implement infra information systems, the Centre for Advanced Information System (CAIS) at Korea Advanced Institute of Science and Technology (KAIST) successfully managed to develop the intelligent campus project and built all necessary infrastructures, that are mandatory prerequisites for the virtual university.

On top of these infrastructures base at KAIST, CAIS has initiated the genuine virtual university project since 1997, and continues to explore the world of virtual university. The CAIS at KAIST has continued its serial virtual university project research, with the knowledge acquired from the intelligent campus project for the last few years. In the process of the development of the project, the usability within the environment of internet was emphasised, since we believed that the usability under the internet client environment, extendibility, and the upgradability was the key trend of current system development.

The project was proposed to import most advanced technologies, evaluate, and apply them to the process of information systems embodiment. The main purpose of KAIST evaluation was to identify and remove all those unstable and risky factors that lie with the importation of new technologies, and to realistically apply those technologies to the information system that embodied at KAIST. The virtual university information system model, the realistic product of this project, thus presents the maximised productivity and efficiency. The product of this project has been reviewed by other research institutions that proved the superiority of the product, and a few universities have already approved to adopt and customise the product as their information systems.

The main goals of the virtual university project are:

i) To establish infrastructure-based application systems such as Electronic Teaching Assistant System, Integrated Workflow System, and Distance Learning System that will motivate virtual educational/administrative activities at KAIST.

ii) To achieve technical perfection in: (a) Client/Server Computing Technique (b) Object-Oriented Methodology Technique (c) Multimedia Technique (d) Database Optimisation Technique (e) Computer Supported Cooperative Work (CSCW) Technique (f) Work-flow Management Technique (g) ATM Network Support Technique (h) Effective Multi-casting Technique (i) System Security Technique (j) Effective Human-Computer Interaction (HCI) Technique (k) Internet/Iinternet Technique and (l) Business Process Re-engineering (BPR) Application Technique.

Launch of intelligent campus project was mainly focused on developing infrastructures, securing database, equipping network and hardware facilities, and implementing basic communication and workflow systems on top of the cumulated database and hardware facilities. Sub-information systems developed are personnel, finance, academic, research, e-mail/BBS, workflow, and library automation system. The virtual university project is instituted to reinforce the intelligent campus foundation by building virtual application systems on top of infra systems constructed.

Certain essential aspect of some well known virtual universities are described below.

Global Virtual University (GVU): The Global Virtual University (GVU) is a virtual university that exists in the cyberspace of the internet. It is a global university accessible to anyone, anywhere, anytime. It is concerned with the future. Its graduates will be professionals with global skills who can work internationally in an information society that will be a better place for their participation. The strength of the GVU lies in a founding faculty of fifty internationally distinguished academics dedicated to radically rethinking the very nature of a university to match the needs of the information society.

The GVU is not supported through any taxation system. It is a commercially based foundation dependent on the fees of its students. The GVU courses are available to anyone with access to the internet. While much of the instructional programme is likely to be text-based, it is becoming possible to give lectures, seminars and tutorials on the internet using audio-conferencing, audio-graphic conferencing, and video-conferencing.

The GVU will have a virtual reality campus on the internet which contain a virtual library, a virtual student union, virtual classrooms and virtual laboratories and a host of other facilities. It will be a place where students and teachers can meet as avatars. The GVU responds to the forces of globalisation and aims to produce a cadre of international professionals with global skills. Globalism in education comes from seeing the content of a particular subject from the multiple perspectives of different cultures and countries. There will be no exclusion of students on any grounds of race, creed, nationality, gender, or age. Students create lifelong social and professional networks during their time at a university.

Usually these are local or national in nature. The GVU will enable students to develop international networks. It will create professionals able to operate at a global level with contacts in many countries. The default language of the GVU is English, but there are no restrictions on the use of any other language. The GVU will offer courses in any language for which there is sufficient demand. Negotiations are taking place to deliver the same course in English, Portuguese and Italian. This is not simply a matter of translating a course into another language. It means looking at a subject from the point of view of different cultures to seek its common essence. The dominant medium for the GVU is the internet. The GVU is negotiating to have a number of centres around the world at places of outstanding cultural interest. These will be centres for GVU meetings and block courses where people from all over the world come together to study, research and play.

Academic direction is on studies that relate to the emerging information society. This implies a focus on the future and on global skills. Special strengths are emerging in such areas as communications, education, translation, English, business and commerce, and information technology. In a world of dynamic change, where too often what is taught and researched is dated before it can be applied, the GVU will be operative, seeking to understand the factors that will affect the information society in order to help shape it.

The GVU was inaugurated by the Rector of the University of Bologna, the oldest university in the world and one that is responsible for the *Magna Charta Universitatum*, a declaration of autonomy and a commitment to the highest standards in teaching and research. The GVU's reputation rests on a founding body of distinguished academics. It is they who take responsibility for academic standards and direction. Every member of the founding faculty is an internationally recognised author and academic and a prophet of the information society in their own country.

The founding faculty can be compared to the editorial board of an encyclopaedia or a research journal. Anybody can submit a course proposal to the GVU but it will require the approval of three members of the founding faculty for the course to be accredited. The founding faculty is responsible for ensuring that standards are maintained which place the GVU at the front rank of universities. Anybody in any country can submit a proposal to teach a course under the aegis of the GVU and if it is accepted they will be remunerated according to the number of students it attracts.

To be accepted the course must be world class and directed to a regional or pan-global market. The proposal will go to three members of the founding faculty for approval and if accepted will become a GVU course and be offered worldwide. Copyright of courses submitted in this way is retained by teachers who are regarded as GVU teaching faculty for as long as they are offering courses. The GVU tries to attract students wanting a global dimension to their knowledge and skills. It is not for people wanting an easy degree. It is for thinkers, those who want to see if they have something special, are innovative, creative, fascinated by the future and the changes that we call information revolution. It is for the self-motivated autonomous learner who can be challenged. Age does not matter, but two kinds of students are envisioned. Those who seek to be skilled global professionals and those who seek knowledge for its own sake.

Courses can be taken for qualification (FQ) which means the student is rigorously examined or not for qualification (NFQ) which means the student did not want to be examined. With other universities, the GVU will create a virtual network. A number of universities have indicated that they would like to be associated with the GVU. Behind this is the idea of globalising university education through the international accreditation of degrees that are an amalgam of courses gained from different but affiliated universities who allow student access to each other's degree programmes via the internet. The

GVU will be a postgraduate university with a strong emphasis on research. Research will mirror teaching, seeking answers to questions about the applications of new technologies.

The GVU will have a research journal on the internet. The founding faculty is the editorial board. The journal will publish doctoral dissertations which will be open for inspection and critique by the global academic community. In this way it will establish and advertise the standards of the GVU and attract those who feel they can match the doctoral requirements. The GVU is governed by a Board of Directors. The Board is composed of a Chairperson, a Secretary and a Treasurer and equal representation of the founding faculty and commercial involvement. It is fundamental axiom of the GVU that the academic and commercial forces involved in its development must be equal. In this way there will be a creative tension between academic purpose and commercial sense. Through the founding faculty, the GVU is currently seeking to affiliate with universities around the world and with professional international organisations. The GVU has a founding faculty of 25 distinguished names, a management team of 25 and extensive experience of delivering courses on the internet. Master's level courses in Teletranslation, Corpus Linguistics, Global Communications and Education on the internet are under development. A Ph.D. programme is ready to be implemented. The GVU will exist on the internet. It will conduct courses and research and be administered and managed and have a social life on the internet.

Michigan Virtual University (MVU): The Michigan Virtual University (MVU) was established in 1998 to meet the specific workforce development education and training needs of Michigan businesses and industries and their current and prospective employees through the innovative use of electronic learning technologies. The MVU was founded by Michigan Governor John Engler and the Michigan Jobs Commission in collaboration with several major industries in the state. The MVU is governed by a board of directors comprising representatives of the Michigan employer community, educational leaders, and representatives of the Michigan Economic Development Corporation.

The MVU was started with an allocation from the Michigan Strategic Fund. In addition, the MVU will generate revenues through fees, grants and contracts with strategic partners. The MVU will not develop courses; instead, it will broker through the state's colleges, universities and private training providers. It will not grant degrees; instead, credentials will be granted by the organisation providing the programme. The primary motivation for creating the MVU was to provide high-quality, convenient, and cost-effective education and training to Michigan's current and prospective employees. Educational institutions' involvement in the MVU will provide access to:

i) Resources to support the preparation of students for work and continuing employment.

ii) Resources and teacher training to assist in the transformation from traditional classroom instruction to learning that can occur any time, any place.

iii) Continuing research on industry employee training needs and distance learning best practices.

iv) Statewide, national and international markets.

v) Collaboratives and cost efficiencies.

The New Jersey Virtual University (NJVU): The New Jersey's public and independent colleges and universities get permission from the Higher Education Technology Infrastructure Fund to accelerate their long-range technology plans and increase their capacity to make higher education more accessible and convenient through distance learning. In the summer of 1998, Governor Christian Whitman called for the creation of a New Jersey Virtual University that builds on this increased capacity.

The New Jersey Virtual University (NJVU) demonstrates how the state's colleges and universities are fully integrating technology to meet workforce training and education needs, as well as the needs of a steadily growing number of high school graduates and adults seeking lifelong learning opportunities. In January 1999, the first phase of NJVU launched, providing a user-friendly index of over 1,000 credit and non-credit courses offered via distance learning by 42 participating public and independent colleges and universities in New Jersey. The index include over 40 complete certificate and degree programmes at the undergraduate and graduate level. Each of the courses and programmes in the virtual university index is offered under the jurisdiction of an individual college or university, which is responsible for all aspects of its distance learning offerings, including the granting of credits, certificates, and degrees. The index allows users to search for desired courses or programmes by institution, subject area, mode of instruction, or other criteria. It enables users to combine criteria to locate the precise offerings that best meet their needs. The index also enables users to link directly to an institution's distance learning web page or online catalogue for specific information regarding courses, admission, registration, cost, and other facts about the institution. The courses and programmes offered by New Jersey higher education institutions respond to the needs of a diverse population of learners requiring flexible timeframes and convenient ways to access education.

As an outgrowth of NJVU, a number of community colleges already participating in the virtual university initiative have joined together to form the New Jersey Virtual Community College Consortium (NJVCCC). Students at any participating community college can register for the shared online courses offered through the consortium. In September 1999, the next phase of NJVU was launched, which focuses on the quality of distance education in New Jersey. It includes an online Faculty Centre that serves as a clearing-house for materials promoting teaching and learning using instructional technology.

The new NJVU website also includes general information about quality in distance learning and information about different types of distance education to help users determine what delivery methods might best meet their educational needs. It includes an interactive questionnaire to help potential students assess whether online courses are right for them. The quality of distance education is the focus of a three-pronged, faculty development initiative proposed by Governor Whitman and supported by the Legislature.

CUX Virtual University: The Corporate University Xchange (CUX) and New Jersey Institute of Technology (NJIT) have announced a partnership to benefit organisations with corporate universities. NJIT has agreed to offer its world-class Webmaster Certificate programme delivered via the web and CD-ROM to members of CUX for a discount tuition fee. In addition, Corporate University Xchange has agreed to produce a conference for the community of webmasters who attend the NJIT programme. The first conference event for webmasters was scheduled for the fourth quarter of 1999. This was the first of many partnerships between Corporate University Xchange and institutions of higher learning as the company expanded its mix of products and services to include world-class accredited online certificate programmes. The CUX Virtual University Webmaster Certificate Programme is composed of three online modules:

i) web author,
ii) web developer, and
iii) website manager.

Each certificate is worth 3 CEUs. Unique to the webmaster programme is the option for graduates to join a webmaster association and receive new content on a quarterly basis, as well as have the opportunity to attend live events produced by Corporate University Xchange.

Clyde Virtual University (CVU): The Clyde Virtual University (CVU) comprises the lecture theatre containing web-based course-ware in a number of subject areas. For copyright reasons the course-ware is only available to users on Clyde Net Metropolitan Area Network. The library holding CVU related material, links to physical libraries within the Clyde Net Institutions and course-ware covering information and study skills. At the CVU assessment hall, students can take online tests either as part of an interactive course-ware module or as stand-alone summative assessments.

The Minnesota Virtual University (MnVU): The Minnesota Virtual University (MnVU) is having more than 85,000 courses from many public and private education providers in Minnesota. The courses on a great variety of subjects delivered via the internet, satellite TV, or on-campus classrooms.

REFERENCES

Bricken, M. and Byrne, C. M., "Summer Children in Virtual Reality: A Pilot Study on Educational Applications of Virtual Reality Technology", In Wexelblat, A (ed.) *Virtual reality: Applications and Explorations.* Academic, Boston, 1993.

Burdea, Grigore and Coiffet, Phillippe, *Virtual Reality Technology*, Wiley-Interscience Publication, 1994.

Cromby, J., Standen, P. and Brown, D., "Using Virtual Reality in Special Education", *VR in the Schools,* 1, 3, 14, 1995.

Ferrington, G. and Loge, K., "Virtual Reality: A New Learning Environment", *The Computing Teacher*, 1992.

Kelly, R. V., The end of cognitive Bulimia, *Virtual Reality Special Report,* 3, 1, 38-50, 1996.

Loeffler, Carl E. and Anderson, Tim, (ed.), *The Virtual Reality Casebook*. Van Nostrand Reinhold, 1994.

Newby, G., Virtual reality. In Williams, M. E. (ed.), *Annual Review of Information Science and Technology*, 1993.

Osberg, K. M., "Virtual Reality and Education: Where Imagination and Experience Meet", *VR in the Schools*, 1995.

Pantelidis, V. S., Virtual Reality in the Classroom, *Educational Technology*, 1993.

Pimentel, Ken and Teixeira, Kevin, *Virtual Reality: Through the New Looking Glass*, Second Edition. Mc Graw-Hill, Inc., 1995.

2
Virtual Learning

The dramatic development of sophisticated and improved technologies has been the driving force behind the widespread embracing of the concept of flexible delivery and the application of the many and varied tools upon which it is based in the field of education. Increasingly institutions and the students and staff working in them are discovering the value of the techniques of resource based learning and the web is being utilised to provide materials for students who are at a distance as well as those who are on campus. Recently numerous tertiary institutions have experimented with the use of online delivery to increasing access to education to a wider audience.

The technology of virtual education can revise or remake the limits, which are given us by our histories and by nature. Distance learning promises more freedom for more people to learn what they choose. It proliferates in the place formerly occupied by the traditional academy. Diverse texts and kinds of information, as well as a multiplicity of consumers and facilitators of learning, increasingly appear in the places formerly held by the canon and the professorate.

Although technology of virtual education is still remote from the ordinary experience of most people, it is nonetheless the dominant means by which human beings are currently remaking the world. The production, transfer, receipt and representation of data are both the tools and the materials of ordering experience and regulating institutions. The technology so prominent and popular in distance learning is the same technology by which we increasingly conduct manufacturing, commerce, medicine, entertainment, even civic and affectionate association, and war.

VIRTUAL CLASSROOMS

Virtual classrooms reflect the escalated commodification of 'real-life' educational practice. The possibilities of the information superhighway touted by the promoters of 'silicon snake oil' have lured many educational institutions to risk educational credibility while exploring the new frontier of cyberspace.

The development of virtual classrooms and universities encapsulates the complexity associated with transforming the solid to the ethereal. The commodification of virtuality for tertiary education relies upon similar meanings becoming associated with this space as are ascribed to the real space of existent campuses. What differs between these spaces is the manner in which communication exchange is undertaken and the compression of time and space that occurs in the virtual environment.

The traditional institutional university structure however has not altered its organisational practices in response to this compression. The monolithic institution continues to utilise traditional Weberian notions of the organisation to contain the unexpected. Efficient workers, business and organisations are configured to possess a economic worth.

The organisation orientated towards virtual space however operates in a compressed space in which vast distance and individual elements of real-life are immediately accessible. The associations of time and space formulated according to the scale of weeks, days, hours, minutes seconds is inappropriate for the virtual organisation requiring instead different configurations of scale and differing relationships to time and space. A reassessment of the economic value measures by these scales is also required. It is for these reasons, that the virtual classroom currently operates as an adjunct to conventional distance learning practices and does not reflect or embrace the full potentials available to the virtual organisation.

Today, universities and the manner in which students receive their tertiary education is changing. Sharing information within an educational context, irrespective of the form it takes, fulfils the specific task of fostering a learning environment and a community of scholars. These issues of pedagogy and the consequent learning outcomes are governed by the rituals of discourse.

This discourse restricts and structures the fluidity in which specified learning objectives can be achieved. These structures and restrictions impact upon the form and context of educational activity by which information is transmitted and received within the classroom. This form of information sharing is however quite different to those information systems operating at an administrative level.

The distinctions that exist for educational practice are more apparent in real-life universities than those which are currently found within the processes of virtual university. These typers of distinction also hallmarks the difference of real-life from a virtual existence. Specific outcomes, beyond the generation of tertiary graduates, must also be accommodated by such universities.

Educational imperatives such as excellence in teaching and international research position must continue to be achieved if the guiding rationale of an academic cultural foundation is to continue. The contemporary practices of universities have dramatically shifted from popular and traditional perceptions of the university. Australian tertiary education and university existence are now positioned within a primarily economic rationale.

The defining goal of educational practice in the late nineties, in Australia, has been flexible learning practices, where information is supplied to the student, now redefined as the client, via an array of mediums. The ritual of discourse in real-life university existence directly informs the construction of virtual universities.

Although educational practice has now branched into many mediums including, written and spoken word, which appear not only via print but which is also recorded, televised and electronically transmitted. This paper will explore the utilisation of virtual space and, more specifically, the spatial adaptation of MUDs (Multi User Dungeons) and MOOs (Multi-user dungeons Object Oriented) as electronic classrooms.

Electronic transmission of text is the new medium being embraced by universities to distribute information to remote, and not-so-remote, students. It contests that regardless of the potential that virtual existence provides for educational practice, if the structured and restrictive organisational practices associated with monolithic and modernist institutions are transposed to this space, the educational potential of the virtual environment will not be realised.

Virtual classrooms currently operate as adjuncts to more conventional distance learning practices. As a result, the educational practices operating in the virtual classroom are an extension of the educational practices of the real-world and do not embrace the full articulation of virtuality that is possible. The traditional and hierarchical organisational structures of universities, and the classroom, when contrasted against the dynamic forms of virtual social space and virtual organisations are less fluid and impede the development of educational possibilities in a virtual environment.

Institutional virtuality, a particular form of virtual presence, incorporates the compression of time and space as part of its organisational formation. Virtual space as an interactive medium and educational tool is most suited to those university services and courses that are more transient or more dynamic in nature. This situation is reflected in the types of information that is being adapted to the virtual face of real-life universities, for example, information relating to academics and their current research, as well as existing courses and administrative advice.

The application of virtual billboards for the dissemination of information has been relatively successful. The challenge for educators has been to successfully transform the experience of interactive real-life learning environments into a virtual learning environment. This task has seen total electronic environments such as MOOs and MUDs being adapted as the shell or outer construct of a textually driven classroom.

Virtual universities as they currently exist are amalgams of electronic rooms and electronically warehoused information. These structures however are still restricted by the traditional organisational models of the monolithic tertiary institution. The traditional and hierarchical structures of the university are reliant upon rules and regulations which stem from older educational practices.

For example, the conceptual framework of the lecture, and the lecture theatres themselves remove any doubt as to who will provide the information from which the student will then be expected to learn. These rooms maximise the hierarchical position of the lecturer and reinforces the students involvement in the machinations of mass education. These relationships construct and reinforce the cultural norms and relationships that hallmark the university and distinguish it from other elements of contemporary society.

The virtual classroom, driven by a lack of corporeality, quickly distorts and challenges these social structures. Virtual universities construct rooms as an environment of exchange for prospective students. These virtual rooms are expected to induce traditional classroom conduct through the cultural associations evoked by a rudimentary simulation of such an environment. However, it is for this reason that the term virtual university is an oxymoron that cannot represent a serious educational organisational structure.

The adaptation of existing real-life information systems does not serve as an adequate model for the fluidity of virtual space. The development of a virtual university is a vastly more complex proposition than the juxtapositioning of the two words. It is a challenge which seeks to translate the solid to the ethereal. Similarly, it is not possible for an organisation operating under modernist frameworks to mimic the structures of commercially orientated virtual organisations. The loose application of extending boundaries through the application of information technology does not automatically predicate a virtual organisation.

The Australian national virtual university, otherwise known as Open Learning Australia, in its current form more closely resembles a series of federated external studies department which operate under the divergent agendas of it is various shareholder institutions. It is not a fluid or interactive entity defining a post-industrial virtual organisation, although some elements could possibly be discerned.

Information flow is heavily governed by the proclivities of academic departments, the operating charter of Open Learning and by university protocol. Until organisational and departmental formations can accommodate the full potential of cyberspace the virtual university will remain a concept or, at best, an information warehouse, in which inappropriate information systems operate across digital boundaries. It is important to position virtual space as a phenomena which is not synonymous with the internet, to appreciate the changes that virtuality imparts upon an information system.

Cyberspace is the spatial phenomena created through the processes of contemporary high technology and is utilised to facilitate human interaction in a manner that is proxy to the capabilities of their bodies. It encompasses the space crafted within video games, the operating theatre of remote surgery and the virtual lathe of Computer-Aided Manufacturing (CAM). Much of the popular media coverage which equates cyberspace with the internet consequently avoids comparative or inclusive considerations of other spaces.

The popularisation of cyberspace seeks to maximise the useability of the environment and has driven the development of automatic and transparent commercial transactions. Information in this context is understood purely in terms of its consumerability and economic value. The hope, if the internet press can be believed, is to reflect a space in which virtual business is maximised by simulating safe shopping environments that are familiar to consumers in the real-world.

Information is reduced in this equation to a coarse dichotomy of objects which are desired and obtainable and those that are not. Beyond this bifurcation of desire, Frampton describes what we see as increasingly polarised between, on one hand, a so-called high-tech approach predicated exclusively upon production and, on the other, the provision of a compensatory facade to cover up the harsh realities of this universal system. This facade, found in the abundance of graphical web browsers, overlays existing information systems and permits organisations to translate existing functions and the rationale of capitalism into virtual space.

Tensions exist between real-space and virtual space which does not permit the mutual interchange of cultural construction between these spaces. This contradiction encapsulates the problematic possibility of creating a total educational infrastructure in virtual space, where the imperative is to achieve higher learning, yet at the same time provide all the institutional prerequisites that are expected of the university.

The virtual university needs to maintain comparative academic legitimacy in order to provide reassurance to both employers and the institutions of higher education. Information, as an object of desire, and existing information systems must conform to existing protocols to achieve legitimisation. This issue, in itself, is of importance with the development of further tertiary based places which add to an already relatively well catered market.

Alternative positions on this situation address the feasibility of these developments and the use of the virtual university as an education medium. A core component of the university is being altered and this necessitates a re-examination of what defines a university as a university. Changes to the systems through which information is disseminated within universities also holds a bearing upon how learning will be undertaken in these new environments.

In cyberspace, information is transferred from one computer to another through dynamic mechanisms that are formed in the complex amalgam of human agency and software. The transference of knowledge in the form of information atoms is the founding rationale for this space. This spatially dislocated culture of exchange is not a unique phenomenon. The maintenance, evolution and dynamism of meaning that formulate social constructions such as gender, power and language all rely upon these exchanges.

Myth, legends and other cultural knowledge require the maintenance of social networks that extend through time and space. The element that differs within these exchanges is the method and medium of communication that are utilised and the form that the exchanged information assumes. Were the form of exchange to be the only significant distinction that was present among these information systems the shift from real to virtual may not represent such a problematic transition.

However, the presence of virtual space is achieved within an environment of compressed of time and space. The social construction of time and space can only exist in relative terms. The division of the conventional clock into twelve is itself an arbitrary construction. It is claimed to be the combination of the four cardinal points with a Babylonian fascination with the number 12. However, there is no day or night in cyberspace to mark the passage of time. Time is instead arbitrarily divided between the two definitive states of being 'logged in' or 'logged out'.

The ability to interact is bound to the technologically defined speeds at which information can be 'physically' transferred across the network. Time and space are compressed in the interplay of maximum information being transacted in minimum time. These transactions are not necessarily technically or interpretatively linear. This is a significant factor in developing approaches to teaching and learning in cyberspace.

Virtual environment and its configuration as a compressed form of time and space is heavily reliant upon the continuous availability of technologically based exchanges. This is an important consideration for defining space as a series of bounded differences. Being virtual is similarly understood with the association of specific notions of time and space. An object in real life is understood in terms of its associated existence, its connection to reality or its mathematical or scientific representation.

A virtual thing has no physical existence, as such, but is made to appear so through software applications. The object in virtual space has no physical or touchable construct although physically can be simulated. The object can be understood to exist in a space that is present through the linking of the computer and telephone. Mackensie Wark describes this specific spatial development by claiming that where we no longer have roots we have aerials. Where we no longer have origins we have terminals.

Spatial positioning, even positioning that is undertaken virtually, is understood in terms of the relationships to objects and to the human self. This understanding of the spatial relationships of cyberspace draw on the notions of humanism and the absence of the Cartesian object. The existence of virtual spaces challenges existing notions of bound space by blurring the edges of reality. The reality that is constructed through those things which dominate the spaces of daily life can be critically presented as meaning-stabilising entities.

The existence of objects in cyberspace do not utilise a physical presence for a social meaning to be determined. This dissolution of the solid and physical also presents a challenge to modernist organisational constructs. The utilisation of MOO's are among recent attempts to overcome the lack of a physical presence within the virtual learning environment. The separation of the individual from the social system reinforces constructs which assert that an ego resides 'within' or somehow inside the individual, whereas, and in distinction, society is somehow positioned outside. In this form of analysis social systems occupy a space outside the individual and are disjointed from a bounded space within the body.

Virtual reality challenges this dualism. The individual's presence and notion of self are not so easily contained while they are interacting in cyberspace. The participant cannot locate their interactions as solely being conducted at the terminal on which they are working, or at the many hundreds of terminals in which their message might be posted to, or along the electronic cables creating global connectivity. This situation makes notions of place increasingly complex as the decreased need for the association of communication with bodily presence challenges representations of physicality and spatiality.

Interactive processes and information exchanges are necessary for the conduct of the business and administration of the university. It is, however, the consumption of material goods and physically bound services that separates the interactivity of organisations located in real-life from those occupying virtual space. Organisations occupying virtual space differ from real-life organisational structures as all forms of exchange assume a common screen-mediated form that is distinct from a physical item but is still being transacted. A virtual organisation irrespective of its motivating force or projected goal relies upon the reciprocity of mutually shared and traversed space to legitimate a virtual presence.

All organisations have an element of virtuality to them. Organisations, as part of their rationale, seek to minimise discrepancies in time and space consensus. The traditional weberian notion of the organisation and its structured efforts to contain the unexpected relies on a calculation of efficiency directly related to time and space. Efficient workers, businesses and organisations are configured to possess a economic worth.

Operations in virtual space however, are conducted in a compressed state in which vast distance and separate aspects of real life spaces are immediately accessible. The associations of time and space formulated according to the scale of weeks, days, hours, minutes and seconds is inappropriate and requires different social constructions of scale and different associations of time to space. A reassessment of economic worth within the measure of these scales is also needed.

Kraft and Truex describe such organisations as possessing many names, "the disparate organisation, the imaginary organisation, the adaptive organisation, the learning organisation, the flexfirm, the agile enterprise, the pulsating organisation, the network organisation and, inevitably, the virtual organisation". These organisational forms are constructed as fluid entities and integrate the knowledge of inevitable and continual change into their structure.

The structures and boundaries of these organisations is always at a point of emergence and realignment. Rigid, set and hierarchical rules and regulations that lay the foundation for large institutions such as universities, are not found in those organisations who are forging a virtual existence. From within the organisation the employee, employer and consumer all carry, convey and perpetuate particular representations of an organisation. Organisational form and its understanding have been dominated by Weber's interpretation of the modern bureaucratic organisation as a process. This process reasserts the continuing mastery by the organisation of the social and physical environment rather than the organisation *per se*. This description suggestions that the rational organisation exists as a form of response to forces which cannot be understood or controlled.

The organisation develops as a series of responses to errors and as a counter-manoeuvre to uncertainty. The organisation then establishes within this process maximum stability and consensus. This position typifies the existence of an 'us' and 'them' organisational form. Constructed so as to position those within a rational organisation as different from those outside it. The members of an organisation understand its machinations from within this bounded existence.

Those experiencing a social reality within the organisation adhere to particular rules of existence for the organisation while those outside this border may not. Maintenance of these boundaries minimises irrationality and unpredictable occurrences within these boundaries. However this process is meant only for those experiencing the social reality found within these boundaries. This positioning problematises the understanding of organisational structure including the university. This view establishes a minimalist perspective and potentially reduces prospects of development. The educational potential is not fully explored by reverting back to existing expectations associated with the usage of space in an educational setting.

Modernity and organisations such as universities seek to perfect themselves through the power of rational thought as the claimed essence of humanity. The university structure as we know it typifies this position making the possibility for the complete transformation of such a large scale institution into a virtual existence appear highly improbable. The ever increasing usage and globally spanning existence of electronic networks of social exchange cannot be not defined through simplistic methods of categorisation.

The development of organisations in virtual space and equally the development of virtual organisations in real-space reveal the contradictions found in organisations constructed within a modernist framework. The virtual organisation is not a fixed entity bound to a physical location or predetermined system. The contradictions of the terms, virtual organisation and virtual university reveals the difficulty in effacing spatial physicality or geographical location from an organisation or bureaucracy which is built around assumptions regarding persistent physicality.

The shift to a virtual existence, where information systems are altered due to a virtual presence, is not simply a smooth transition from existing modernist bound rules and regulations. Information does not have the same protocols that both limit and encompass it in the geographically and physically bound existence of real-life. It is for this reason information in a virtual environment both for educational and business purposes can be utilised differently.

A Virtual Classroom Model

Various virtual classroom systems have been developed so far. Examples of representative virtual classroom systems include Virtual Classroom at New Jersey Institute of Technology, Virtual Classroom at Cornell University, Collaboratories at the US Department of Energy, Albatross Project at National Chiao Tung University, Taiwan, and Interactive Remote Instruction System at Old Dominion University. Each system may have its own features differing from others. They all have one common goal—to educate students who are motivated to learn but are blocked by their geographical locations and/or working schedules.

However, two areas that face almost all virtual classroom systems that provide real-time interactivity with students over the internet but have not been given due attention are:

i) Controlled activities for students who are out of the reach of direct supervision from the instructor, and

ii) Coordinated interaction among participants while using audio tools for interactive dialogues.

The model here given is named as Virtual Classroom Over the Internet (VCOIN). This model features a centralised mouse control mechanism to provide the instructor with the capability to call remote students' attention to class and to synchronise class activities, and a First-Come First-Serve (FCFS) floor control to regulate participants engaged in audio conferencing in an orderly fashion. The major features of VCOIN are:

i) Uses the internet as its networking infrastructure for information distribution.

ii) Uses existing video/audio conferencing tools for interactive real-time communication.

iii) Uses standard web browsers for graphical user interfaces.

iv) Employs a mouse control technique to prevent students from conducting unauthorised surfing in cyberspace.

v) Employs a floor control algorithm that allows the instructor centralised floor control while students are allowed to access the floor in an FCFS fashion.

vi) Introduces the concept of virtual experimenter.

vii) Provides a chat tool to enable interactive text-based communications between the instructor and the students.

Several VCOIN trial sessions have been conducted using multiple computer labs that are interconnected via a 100 Mbps Ethernet-type campus backbone. VCOIN uses Netscape Navigator for its user interface. VCOIN builds into itself a unique feature of checking and controlling the student activities at a remote place. This feature is called Mouse Detect. Consider a scenario in which the instructor expects all students to pay attention to what he/she is demonstrating. The instructor will then request the students to place their mouse in a specific area on their screen. VCOIN will detect these activities and notify the instructor of the students' current status.

In VCOIN, a combination of a centralised control (for instructor) and an FCFS (for students) is employed. The instructor always has the authority to speak. A student user is allowed to speak only when he/she is given the permission of floor control by the instructor. This type of control is necessary to avoid chaos and confusion in a conferencing environment and it helps to structure the interaction and reduce the bandwidth requirement. The floor control algorithm used in VCOIN is an FCFS algorithm for students and centralised control for the instructor. A student has to submit the request from his/her VCOIN interface. On the other hand, if the instructor would like to release the floor control from a student who currently has it, he/she would have to click on "Release floor" button on the VCOIN interface. The users who wish to take the floor control submit their request to the controller. The controller puts the request of each user into the FIFO queue. Because the conferencing application is used in a virtual classroom environment. Users have three options are given below:

i) Request floor control,
ii) Release floor control, and
iii) Quit conference.

When the user having the floor control requests for release of floor, the controller pops the first element off the FIFO queue and give the floor control to it. The conference application will then allow that user to access the shared resource. If a user requests to quit the conference the floor control mechanism would remove the corresponding User ID from the current user list. This feature is used to provide hands-on experience with the material covered in class. It is implemented as a Java applet that can run on any Java-enabled system.

CHALLENGES IN VIRTUAL LEARNING

Challenges of virtuality confront both the non-profit and the for-profit providers of most services, including learning services. Indeed, the internet is changing the competitive environment in which both non-profit and for-profit providers of postsecondary learning services operate today. How one deal with these challenges depends on one's point of view.

The anyplace/anytime technologies that enables virtual learning services become highly pertinent in the post-baccalaureate and adult education market, mainly because of the increased convenience and access offered to the student by virtual instruction. This is not to say that virtual technologies cannot be used to enhance the traditional undergraduate experience; they can. But the traditional residential experience is not solely about the transfer of knowledge.

Classroom-based activities, especially in the major colleges and universities, do support knowledge transfer and acculturation into a discipline or profession—entrance into the guild, so to speak—but the total residential undergraduate experience has another important component: social acculturation, helping young people become civilised, enjoy personal growth, achieve a degree of maturity, and become good citizens. The post-baccalaureate education and training market is growing rapidly in response to the lifelong learning needs of the emerging knowledge economy and the catalytic boost provided by new, nimble competitors that outsource infrastructure and related instructional technology support in order to create virtual instructional programmes without large investments in bricks and mortar and support staff.

In the adult/post baccalaureate market, the 'audience' for educational services changes; it puts a premium on convenience and access. Imagine a box divided into four quadrants by two perpendicular vectors: one is geography or place, from someplace to anyplace; the second is time, from sametime to anytime. So, there are four quadrants: someplace/

sametime, someplace/anytime, anyplace/sametime; and anyplace/anytime. Virtual learning opportunities are those enabled by the technologies that fall in the space defined by anytime/anyplace. If you look at the learning opportunities enabled by anyplace/anytime instruction, you see possibilities for providing education and training that is more learner-centric, more appropriate for this post-baccalaureate market, which really values convenience and extended access.

The traditional, brick-and-mortar campuses are really struggling with the extent to which they should offer virtual curricula as opposed to enhancing place/time bound curricula through the use of virtual technologies. For the traditional campus, it is the issue of how to achieve the right clicks-and-mortar balance between bricks-and-mortar programming and opportunities for virtual programming. But if you look at the competitive issues facing higher education, you find that they derive from the possibilities of anytime/anyplace service delivery models and from the leveraging of partnerships enabled by the internet.

Virtual service is a service that is delivered dominantly in anyplace/anytime mode. The basic assumption in web terms is that the service receiver, whether an organisation or an individual, has an internet connection and has access to that connection almost any time. The service provider has no responsibility for providing that access or the PC that attaches to the Net, that is, has no particular facilities responsibility.

Historically, higher education has been focused on the notion of a learned society—a learned-centric, faculty-centric, library-centric institution. But we are now in a continuous process of transformation of adapting anyplace/anytime technologies to make higher education more learner-centric, or customer or student-centric—whether in support of traditional someplace/sametime instruction or to create anyplace/anytime instructional programmes. Virtual technologies really shift the emphasis to the service receivers, who are beginning to demand more convenience and easier access, and technology allows the delivery of these services. We have a ways to go in traditional higher education, particularly if we want to reach the goal of a learning-centric institution. It is not just about convenience and access—it is also about the learning outcome of the experience.

A lot of current faculty concerns—coursework being placed on the web and who owns the copyright to it, are really misplaced. Learning has never been just about content. There is too much emphasis placed on content as though every faculty member has built a course from scratch or has written a textbook. In fact, the faculty's role has been about other things: selecting, sequencing and organising the course materials; adding value in the form of guiding self study, giving and grading tests, assigning papers; and, especially, facilitating the shared discovery of knowledge—the classroom as a seminar, not as a lecture. Reducing these three roles to the first two of providing material and giving tests turns the process into a correspondence course. The missing piece is collaborative learning —facilitating that seminar-like experience and encouraging learning in a group. It is one of the needs of the online environment: how to create a collaborative learning environment.

The cultural values that shape the traditional general educational experience designed for 18 to 22-year-old students and apprentice scholars are, appropriately, different from those that shape post-baccalaureate professional education and development. Mixing the two cultures, along with competing common-good and profit motives, often results in controversy rather than results. The separate spin-off entities that some institutions are creating to provide virtual instruction for the post-baccalaureate professional education market are also vehicles for capital appreciation and for rewarding excellent instructors for successful instructional innovations in ways that their salaries cannot. Another reason for spinning off separate organisations to create and offer virtual education or training programmes lies in the need to be nimble and cost effective in the face of the new competition that is entering the post-baccalaureate professional education market. That new competition is not burdened with ongoing investments in bricks and mortar and in internal service bureaus/bureaucracies that are resistant to change and that are not accustomed to being held accountable for delivering measurable outcomes on a schedule.

The traditional resource model is input-oriented, not output-oriented. The new breed of competitor, often outsources many of these services and even its faculty and credentialing programmes from other organisations in the interest of time to market and as a means to avoid costly investments in infrastructure and salaries and training for expert services that are scarce in today's labour market—technical support professionals, webmasters, instructional designers, and so on. With no baggage to carry, spin-off entities can build their educational services by appropriately mixing intellectual resources from their parent organisations with virtual operating services acquired from other non-profit and for-profit partner organisations in order to get to market quickly and cost effectively. This is another dimension to virtuality: it is how the services are provided, whether they are internally provided or outsourced to gain the leverage of the economy-of-scale investments and expertise of external partner organisations.

Institutions of higher education exist so that students will not have to search out tutors; colleges are brokers in that business and accredit the outcome. As long as companies and colleges have to create internal operating services necessary to the delivery of their core products and services—that is overhead services like accounting and legal departments or admissions and registrars' offices or IT divisions—they become larger and less nimble.

When the internet is entered into the equation, we find that many of these services can be bought on the open market cost effectively and with little friction in managing the resulting service contracts, whether they represent infrastructure, e-commerce or the Application Service Provider (ASP) model of hosting and supporting e-learning programmes.

In the virtual service model, many higher education institutions are outsourcing their infrastructure and externally obtaining other service functions necessary to deliver their curricula, enabling them to focus on their core intellectual functions. In the long run, it is cheaper, faster to market, and more agile for institutions of higher education to contract for these services rather than to make the capital investments and hire the necessary expertise themselves. Eduprise hosts instructional management systems, provides 24 × 7 support services, including a 1-800 help desk service, all on multiple platforms. Then, we add web integration services and portal services. And we provide strategic and tactical planning, instructional design, course development, and outcome evaluation services to help the client organisation maximise its return on investment in virtual technologies. This frees the client to capitalise on its intellectual assets—the expertise of its faculty and its libraries in the case of a traditional college or university—without additional capital or human resource investments to design and implement an appropriate e-learning environment.

E-learning is an opportunity for traditional institutions of higher education to leverage their intellectual capital in new ways. It gives some institutions an opportunity to use their intellectual capital to attract new audiences and even to attract companies willing to make an investment in developing that audience as a for-profit market. Together, we can have a new, for-profit venture that we can look to for capital appreciation. That's part of the idea at some, mostly brand-name institutions. There's a whole culture behind traditional higher education that makes it very difficult for traditional institutions to move quickly.

Today, the adult and post-baccalaureate learning markets are very practical and became more attractive to faculty members. This is a new venue for teaching and learning, which offers an opportunity for instructors to supplement their traditional income base. This new for-profit venture can carry additional monetary rewards for talented and interested instructors—just as research grants have carried additional monetary reward for interested and talented researchers in areas of inquiry that present opportunities for external funding.

Some talented faculty members pursue grants, which bring in funding for them and their institutions and enhance their status in the prevailing incentive structure. The new virtual-campus constructs, whether created for-profit or non-profit, can give other talented faculty members an opportunity for additional income, sometimes even corporate equity, in an endeavour that can also serve the best interest of their institutions, whether that is in reaching and serving new audiences for a profit or for other reasons related to revenues.

A large part of the demand for e-learning does have strong vocational overtones, explicitly the market for virtual adult and post-baccalaureate programmes. The problem lies in not recognising that we are often trying to do two very different things with virtual technologies within an institution rooted in one set of values—on the one hand, strengthen traditional higher education for 18 to 22-year-olds and would-be faculty members and, on the other hand, deliver virtual learning to the adult and post-baccalaureate markets. These are two different goals, each with its own different but equally valid set of values.

Throughout the 1970s and 1980s, technical innovation brought increasingly diverse and more powerful technological tools into schools. These technologies were typically text-based, locally networked or stand-alone computer-assisted instruction applications. The combination of computation, connectivity, visual and multimedia capacities, and speed have radically changed the potential for technologies in schooling.

Tensions of virtual learning arise because students and teachers now reach out over huge distances to engage each other in learning. The very technology which allows them to connect also swells the tensions always present in education between freedom and control, authenticity and acquiescence. These distances are spatial, temporal, and multitudinously cultural. Learning in virtual reality makes possible an efficiently abstract relationship between teacher and student. Generically professional teachers dispense and evaluate the learning of generically dutiful students. Individual differences of curiosity, ability or circumstance do not count.

Academic cheating on the internet is a serious problem. Of course, prior to digitally constructed reality, students found plenty of ways to make themselves appear to know that which they did not. In answer to the professorial desire for control, students can effectively dissimulate the appearance of learning. Malicious or not, academic cheating is a way to free or distance one's authentic self from the work and commitment required by professors. Internet education simply makes this effort much easier than ever. Virtual but inauthentic learning is now commonplace, profitable and, so far, legally protected. Websites, such as "Evil House of Cheat", and "school-sucks", at least acknowledge a distinction between one's own learning and someone else's. It is ironic that when students fail to cheat successfully, we are then given the opportunity to make a genuine connection with them. We can talk with them about what they had hoped to do, what they desired, and especially, what they feared. One would never choose or need to programme such uncomfortable moments into a completely planned virtual education.

Courseware can be programmed to allow for a limited variety and number of predetermined paths of interaction between student, academic material and teacher. People who rarely, if ever, have any communication with students sometimes design such courseware. In this flow of knowledge transmission, teachers can largely administrate the delivery of the material and certify the results generated by an automated learning evaluation instrument. However, matching these techniques of professorial control, students can deploy a variety of devices to reproduce responses they know will pass.

Indeed, students can even shrewdly simulate authenticity—the authenticity of imperfection—by using ready-made work which is not first class or to which they can add little slips. Thus, students have their own manipulations in this regime of knowledge as power.

Virtual education fulfils several new tendencies in university mass education. Some critical theorists have optimistically envisioned flexible mixed mode methods and autonomous learning in a new generation or post-Fordist model of distance education. Students and teachers can make good use of the possibilities of sophisticated communication technology to create opportunities for genuine interaction and mutual inquiry. However, even these theorists worry that such opportunities in both production and consumption of learning materials will not be widely accessible, due to the customary organisational hierarchy of academic institutions. It is the very lure of power offered by virtual reality that may well hold teachers and students within the regime of control.

Economically, distance learning, like the often-caricatured version of lecture-hall teaching in the multiversity, can be extraordinarily cost-efficient. A huge number of students, supplied with identical textbooks or courseware, can be serviced by a tiny number of teachers. In this way, university education perfectly applies tenets of post-industrial productivity.

The virtual university can project the reach of professorial power to literally any point on the globe. No longer limited by the lectern rising at the front of an auditorium-sized classroom, professors and the expertise they have deemed canonical can now be world-class. This type of education, in its most perfect form, reduces learning and teaching to mere control and to instrumental behaviours.

REFERENCES

Alcord, B., and Wittgen, A., "The Authority to Think: The Student-centred Classroom", *Contemporary Education*, 61(2), 1990.

Brooksfield, S.D., *The Skilful Teacher: On Technique, Trust, and Responsiveness in the Classroom,* San Francisco, CA: Jossey-Bass, 1990.

Burow-Flake, E., Kocher, D., Reiser, A., *Changing Students, Changing Classroom Landscapes: Meeting the Challenge in the Small Liberal Arts Institution,* in L. Lloyd (ed.), *Teaching with Technology, Rethinking Tradition,* Medford, NJ: Information Today, Inc., 2000.

Cohen, J. A., Castner, M. H., *Technology and Classroom Design: A Faculty Perspective*, in L. Lloyd (ed.), *Teaching with Technology, Rethinking Tradition*, Medford, NJ: Information Today, Inc., 2000.

Comeaux, P., "The Impact of an Interactive Distance Learning Network on Classroom Communication", *Communication Education*, 41(4), pp. 353-361, 1995.

Duhaney, D., Technology and the Educational Process: Transforming Classroom Activities, *International Journal of Instructional Media*, 27(1), pp.67-72, 2000.

Jorn D., Hill Duin A. and Wahlstrom B., 'Designing and Managing Virtual Learning Communities' *IEEE Transactions of Professional Communication*. 39(4), 1996.

Hiltz, R. S., *The Virtual Classroom*, Norwood, NJ: Ablex, 1995.

Maddox, C. C., *The World Wide Web and School Culture: Are they Compatible?*, in D. L. Johnson, C. D. Maddux, and L. Lieu, (eds.), *Using Technology in the Classroom*, New York: The Haworth Press, 1997.

McHenry, L., and Bozik, M., "Communicating at a Distance: A Study of Interaction in a Distance Education Classroom", *Communication Education*, 44(4), pp. 362-371, 1995.

Pantelidis, V. S., Virtual Reality in the Classroom, *Educational Technology*, 1993.

Velayo, R. S., "Supplementary Classroom Instruction via Computer Conferencing", *Educational Technology*, 1994.

Wilson, A., "Instructional Multimedia in the Math Classroom and Beyond", *Paper presented at the Annual Conference of the American Mathematical Association of Two-year Colleges*, Tulsa, OK, November 3-6, 1994.

Woodruff, M and Mosby, J., A brief description of videoconferencing, Videoconferencing in the classroom and library, 1996.

Zhang, S., and Fulford, C.,"Are Interaction Time and Psychological Interactivity the Something in the Distance Learning Television Classroom?" *Educational Technology*, 34(6), pp. 58-64, 1994.

3
Virtual Teaching and Student Engagement

An understanding of the techniques and protocols of online teaching and learning and the processes of both the design of new and the conversion of old courses has become essential for academics, as universities throughout the world embrace alternative delivery methods in response to the globalisation of education. Multimedia and computer-based simulations can elucidate abstract concepts and help students participate in their learning. Online teaching should be linked to specific learning objectives so that they can be used as valuable tools.

Online teaching provides students with active learning experiences. It helps students to understand abstract or complicated ideas. It provides useful applications of theoretical ideas connecting students with other professionals in the field Teachers should use this activity as a springboard. They should know their students, curriculum and facilities. They should be creative with your level of computer access. Many of the pages can be printed out and read off-line. Teachers should use library resources that could be scanned or drawn through a computer paint programme.

Schedules and commuting students often make it difficult to meet face-to-face for group work. Information communication technologies can provide unique strategies to promote convenient collaboration. In the same way that one may prefer maths to literature, students may also develop preferences regarding the way they learn about these disciplines. During the course, the teacher may want feedback from their students on their expectations, their progress, or their satisfaction in the course. Bridging the gap between in-class lectures and real-world experience can be a challenge. If the teacher is looking for ways to develop lecture materials more efficiently, engage the audience more fully, or disseminate the presentation outside the classroom, several tools can help.

Vibrant student discussion can be a crucial part of learning, but is sometimes limited by class time. In a large class, an open discussion may be impossible to manage. E-mail and electronic discussion tools extend opportunities for interaction, provide students with a chance to contribute, and allow students to compose their thoughts in writing.

E-mail and a suite of other tools in this category can help the teacher disseminate information widely and coordinate group discussions. Create threaded newsgroups that facilitate continued conversation about course material outside of class time. Students can view and contribute to newsgroups from the web as well as from the pine-based interface. Encourage students to widen their spectrum of experience with course materials by contacting other professionals via electronic discussion.

An online course should be inductive and interactive. An on-line course can add multicultural and international dimensions to the subject matter. To really encourage student's use of a supplemental website, include a 'guest' account that students can use. If the teacher is planning on monitoring individual student's use of online material, let the students know this up front. If the student view differs from the instructor's view, create a student account that the teacher can use to verify appearance and behaviour of new material prior to releasing it to the students. The need to check external links regularly for functionality, accuracy, validity and content.

If materials are posted online, it is much easier for students who must travel, who are sick, or otherwise unable to get to regular lecture periods, to get the learning materials that they would otherwise miss. This reduces student panic and the number of calls to the instructor. Some libraries provide an electronic reserve service wherein they will post required readings online. Expect and plan for problems, such as students who cannot access their email, students getting locked up halfway through a timed online quiz, etc. Be flexible and have a backup. If the teacher is suspicious of the reported problem, most courseware programmes include student-tracking routines that can be used to investigate and verify some types of problems.

Teachers should create something like a 'bootcamp' that introduces students to all the tools they will be using during the course and explain what each tools is for, how it can be used, variations, time-saving tips, give examples and provide practice opportunities. They should also create a small sample course which students can access to see whether they have the necessary software, connection speed, and computer skills to tackle an entire on-line course before signing up for one. The teachers should:

a) create a website where students can check their own readiness for on-line instruction.

b) spellout communication policies, expectations, and responsibilities for both students and instructors in the course syllabus.

c) designate a portion of the main page for announcements. Use a different colour background for the announcement section so that it stands out better. Post reminders, test feedback, encouraging remarks and similar things.

d) create private discussion forums for each group so that they can communicate with one another without the entire class being able to read their comments.

e) schedule chat rooms and weekly bulletin boards that students must respond to keep them on task and in touch.

f) schedule chat room office hours for evenings. During the day students will be at work, school, etc.

g) begin discussions with questions that you know most students can answer correctly. Provide lots of positive feedback to encourage participation.

h) keep a log of office hour chat room discussions. Edit the log and replace each student's name with the word 'student'.

i) create a frequently asked question (FAQ) list that is accessible from the main web page. When you receive more than two e-mails asking for the same information/ clarification, add a hint or explanation to the FAQ list.

j) create bulletin board works well for discussion of issues and peer critique of scholarly writing, students need to be given points for the participation and guidelines for what is appropriate discussion on the bulletin board. Assign an article to read and request students to post a short summary on the course bulletin board. Assign different articles to different groups but request only one summary per group. Students must also submit an answer with each question. The incentive is that if their question is selected, they should be able to get full points.

k) create several discussion forums, each on a different topic. Have students self-select one or two to participate. Each discussion group must summarise their discussions in two weeks.

l) have students submit terms and explanations to be included in the course glossary.

m) divide the class into groups and assign each group a different course topic to teach to the rest of the class.

n) have students recommend websites that supplement the topics being covered.

o) create a list of questions that match the learning objectives for each module. If you want students to be able to recall specific facts or definitions, teach mnemonic devices and provide numerous self-practice drills. If you want students to understand or comprehend particular relationships or events, ask them to describe or explain, compare or contrast, or summarise ideas. If the goal is for students to be able to apply rules, formulae or procedures to unfamiliar data or situations, then ask them to demonstrate this, possibly with online exams, test cases provided online, or by performing some sort of exercise offline and reporting back. The highest cognition category is critical thinking or problem solving.

Teachers need to flesh out a power-point slides slide with all the information that would normally accompany it in a lecture. This can be done with an audio recording as well as with text passages. Where practical, pair learning goals with self-study drill on every lesson page. Focus on no more than a handful of important points in each lesson. If necessary, break a lesson into several separate pages, each having a key point. Use graphics to help convey an idea. One or two carefully selected, clear images are generally sufficient. Make visual diagrams that show the connections/relationships between ideas. This is easily done with power-point or simple drawing packages. These images are a simple blend of shapes, lines, colour and text.

Have an accompanying text passage or audio clip that explains the concepts and relationships represented. Such images break-up text passages and provide useful frameworks for processing information. Remember that lesson pages will probably be printed out. Check that they printout legibly, within regular margins, and so on. Format lesson pages for quick scanning as well as easy reading. Use bullets. Use indents to create left and right margins. Maintain a consistent informational structure and page layout for lesson pages.

The teachers should include lots of short self study drills or even quizzes that give student's a chance to practise. Allow students multiple attempts at a quiz, however, keep only the first score. This lets students go back and practise or review while at the same time discouraging cheating. Since the first attempt is the grade kept on record, students cannot use their first attempt to preview questions for a later real attempt. Make sure to tell your students how the scores are kept. To create a large question bank, get questions from previous semesters' midterms and final exams.

While entering a title for a question, include some type of notation that indicates the question format. For example, preface with a P for paragraph, S for short answer, MI for multiple choice one answer, MM for multiple choice with many answers, C for calculated and M for matching. This will be useful when you are creating your quizzes. To check whether questions have been entered properly in website, create a single quiz that contains all the questions you wish to check. Either assign a password that only you know or create a release condition so that only your dummy student account can access the quiz. Make sure that question titles are included on the quiz and that both scores and answers are provided as feedback. Login as a student and go to the quiz. Submit it without answering any question. Review the results, checking that the appropriate answers are being graded as correct.

Online testing methods can be used are as varied as those used in any teaching and learning environment however some concerns were raised concerning aspects of collaborative work, the nature of the assessment task used and the security issue.

Advances in IT and the power and allure of the WWW means that while traditional classroom style delivery is still the most prolific, it is decreasing. Organisations are still cautious, as to how much of the delivery should be technology based. Video and computer-based training products have been available and popular for some time adding value when used appropriately. Many companies are now saying that just-in-time training using the WWW allows an information-pull philosophy which lets staff access training materials in their own time, at their own place and in a location of their choice.

The most effective type of WWW training include a wide variety of hyperlinks reference material. Tools such as Sun's Java and Macromedia's Schockwave add interest rather than educational value. Virtual training colleges such as virtual university and/or global internet campus http://vetweb.net.au now exist although there is no physical location.

As time and resources became scarcer training has become much more target-specific allowing staff to focus their time and attentions on what they actually need to know at a time that they need to know it, i.e., just-in-time and/or just-what's needed. Materials that can be used later as a refresher and reference tool and that have a series of self-paced exercises provide the most flexibility. Given the fact that the content has to be created anyway for traditional face-to-face delivery, some organisations are looking at maximising their training dollar by looking to the WWW to provide the most flexible delivery possible. Cyber training allows for non-linear based programmes allowing staff to jump around the programme to suit their own needs.

To overcome technology-based problems we should ensure that all students have access to first class technology support provided by people who know more than just what buttons to press. Support personnel needed to have an understanding of how the technology works and how it can be best utilised on on-line learning environments.

The students need to be trained in the basic use and operation of the technology before they start and this is often best achieved by face-to-face instruction at the start of session. As a good rule of thumb, it was suggested by many that problems are minimised by designing the web interface to the lowest common denominator in terms of available technology.

Related to this aspect is the equity issue of student access. Some universities have dial-in access, for students but most students will need access to a private internet service provider. Participants were pointed to websites which had attempted to address this issued utilising alternative delivery formats and there were many participants who were willing to share their experience, triumphs and disappointments having followed the pathway of providing standard hardware configurations to the registered students in their courses.

The most significant challenges for those running online courses is the silent student. Ensuring that the students engage in the learning is closely related to the degree of interactivity fostered between students and their peers as well as between the students and the instructor. Success in the latter is dependent upon an instructors commitment to providing rapid feedback to submitted tasks and posed questions as well as regular personal checking in online. Such commitment provides an incentive for all students to be active and enthusiastic. There will however always be a proportion of students who for one reason or another, do not regularly check in or take active roles in the online environment.

Participants in the discussion provided many suggestions to help overcome the dropout problem ranging from a 'quiet email message' to those concerned, to personal phone calls when the situation became more serious. Active participation however is a function of how well the environment is structured and the need to provide well structured courses in which the style and mode of presentation is varied was emphasised in many postings.

One common theme throughout the posting was the recognition of the need to consider carefully the design and structuring of on-line courses, particularly those, which-already existed in a traditional format. Content cannot be simply placed on the web. Time and effort must be spent in considering the resources and structure needed to best present the course in the new environment.

Redeveloping a course for online delivery is not an easy or short process. Likewise managing such courses once they are up and running is not easy. More students means more time on-line, which means more of the instructors' time is spent communicating with individuals and groups. A number of participants in the discussion related the success of such mechanisms as subject mailing lists, web-based archives, announcement spaces and the like at reducing their overall workload. An analysis of these points identifies the following key areas of concern:

a) Logistical concerns such as aspects of student access financial resources and the availability of trained personnel who can develop and implement instruction online.
b) Instructional content concerns such as its appropriateness for the delivery mechanism being used, the format of presentation used and the various media utilised.
c) Management of delivery concerns which focus on aspects of achieving individualisation of instruction. Facilitation of interaction between students and the students and the instructor and the effective management of large numbers. An important and critical aspect of the management of the process is the need to track and measure student progress accurately and effectively. Related to this is the area of process security and feedback, which many practitioners see as a major issue to be addressed.

Development, implementation and management of online teaching and learning environments are costly and time consuming. The number of courses being offered online is expanding rapidly and at the same time the knowledge base of what determines an effective online subject is also expanding rapidly. Several issues recognised as critical to success have not changed since the earliest experiments. It cannot be presumed that online subjects will take less time to teach. Considerable planning and organisation is required and support teams are necessary for successful implementation. An online environment can provide a more flexible learning environment for many students and teachers, however many issues need to be addressed by institutions if courses are to be successful.

Instructors often comment that the focused preparation required by virtual teaching improves their overall teaching and empathy for their students. The challenges posed by virtual education are countered by opportunities to:

i) Reach a wider student audience
ii) Meet the needs of students who are unable to attend on-campus classes
iii) Involve outside speakers who would otherwise be unavailable
iv) Link students from different social, cultural, economic, and experiential backgrounds.

While adapting virtual instruction, the core content remains basically unchanged, although its presentation requires new strategies and additional preparation time. Some suggestions for planning and organising a distance delivered course are given below.

i) Begin the course planning process by studying virtual education research findings. There are several research summaries available.
ii) Before developing something new, check and review existing materials for content and presentation ideas.
iii) Analyse and understand the strengths and weaknesses of the possible delivery systems available to you not only in terms of how they are delivered, but in terms of learner needs and course requirements before selecting a mix of instructional technology.
iv) Hands-on training with the technology of delivery is critical for both teacher and students. Consider a pre-

class session in which the class meets informally using the delivery technology and learns about the roles and responsibilities of technical support staff.

v) At the start of class initiate a frank discussion to set rules, guidelines, and standards. Once procedures have been established, consistently uphold them.

vi) Make sure each site is properly equipped with functional and accessible equipment. Provide a toll-free "hot-line" for reporting and rectifying problems.

vii) If course materials are sent by mail, make sure they are received well before class begins. To help students keep materials organised, consider binding the syllabus, handouts, and other readings prior to distribution.

viii) Start off slowly with a manageable number of sites and students. The logistical difficulties of distant teaching increase with each additional site.

Efforts should be made to adapt the delivery system to best motivate and meet the needs of the students, in terms of both content and preferred learning styles. Consider the following strategies for meeting students' needs:

i) Assist students in becoming both familiar and comfortable with the delivery technology and prepare them to resolve the technical problems that will arise.

ii) Make students aware of and comfortable with new patterns of communication to be used in the course.

iii) Learn about students' backgrounds and experiences. Discussing the instructor's background and interests is equally important.

iv) Be sensitive to different communication styles and varied cultural backgrounds.

v) Remember that students must take an active role in the distance delivered course by independently taking responsibility for their learning.

vi) Be aware of students' needs in meeting standard university deadlines, despite the lag time often involved in rural mail delivery.

Effective virtual teaching requires the enhancement of existing skills, rather than developing new abilities. Special attention should be given to the following:

i) Assess the amount of content that can be effectively delivered in the course.
ii) Be aware that student participants will have different learning styles. Some will learn easily in group settings, while others will excel when working independently.
iii) Diversify and pace course activities and avoid long lectures. Intersperse content presentations with discussions and student-centred exercises.
iv) Humanise the course by focusing on the students, not the delivery system.
v) Consider using a print component to supplement non-print materials
vi) Use short, cohesive statements and ask direct questions, realising that technical linkages might increase the time it takes for students to respond.
vii) Develop strategies for student reinforcement, review, repetition, and remediation.

Using effective interaction and feedback strategies will enable the instructor to identify and meet individual student needs while providing a forum for suggesting course improvements. To improve interaction and feedback:

i) Use pre-class study questions and advance organisers to encourage critical thinking and informed participation on the part of all learners.
ii) Arrange telephone office hours using a toll-free number. Set evening office hours if most of your students work during the day.

iii) Integrate a variety of delivery systems for interaction and feedback, including one-on-one and conference calls, fax, e-mail, video, and computer conferencing.

iv) Contact each site every week if possible, especially early in the course. Take note of students who don't participate during the first session, and contact them individually after class.

v) Use pre-stamped and addressed postcards, out-of-class phone conferences, and e-mail for feedback regarding course content, relevancy, pace, delivery problems, and instructional concerns.

vi) Use an on-site facilitator to stimulate interaction when distant students are hesitant to ask questions or participate.

vii) Call on individual students to ensure that all participants have ample opportunity to interact. At the same time, politely but firmly discourage individual students or sites from monopolising class time.

viii) Make detailed comments on written assignments, referring to additional sources for supplementary information.

STUDENT'S ENGAGEMENT

Conceiving of software as electronic texts would permit teachers and researchers to borrow constructs from investigations of literacy for application to instructional technology. They are information structures stored by and accessible through nonprint electronic media. Teachers and researchers could examine and support how readers use rhetorical and experiential knowledge and evaluative reasoning to construct personal meanings in transactions with electronic texts, such as educational software.

Readers build personal knowledge by exploring alternative meanings in textual representations. Such meaning-making requires interpretive skills sensitive to text structure, context, and perspective. High literacy as literate thinking, is a process of personal meaning-making, possessing three essential elements. They are:

i) A sensitivity to the structure of text and an ability to evaluate and interpret the significance of its forms;
ii) A sophisticated view of and skill with the possibilities of interpretation, that interpretation of a document may evolve over time, that more than one interpretation is possible, that perspective can influence understanding of text, and that interpretation from multiple perspectives enhances understanding of text;
iii) An awareness of personal intellectual, perceptual, and emotional associations evoked by transactions with text and an ability to interweave these associations with interpretations, evoking insights into one's prior personal experiences.

High literacy as an act of intentional learning involving problem-solving and self-regulatory skills deployed by complex executive structures. It is characterized by cognitive flexibility, spontaneous, adaptive restructuring of schemes to solve problems of comprehension and application in the reading of texts. Aesthetic reading emphasizes the sensations, images, feelings, and emotional and intellectual associations evoked during reading. Efferent reading, by contrast, concerns "what is to be retained for later use, such as information, directions for action, summation, or publicly verifiable facts".

The notion of literate thinking is also influenced by Langer's definition of four stances in "literary thinking". In one stance, a reader seeks a general sense of what a text is about, relying on prior knowledge and experience and document features to generate general impressions—a holistic stance. In another stance, a reader explores understandings of a text, asking questions to extend those understandings into horizons of possibility—an exploratory stance. Third, a reader uses emerging understandings to reflect on his or her personal life—a reflective stance. A fourth stance is that of the critic, one who evaluates emerging understandings, characteristics of the text, and one's experience of the text—a critical stance. A reader can move among stances in any order.

High literacy entails high engagement in interpretive acts. We define engagement as the mobilisation of cognitive, affective, and motivational strategies for interpretive transactions with text. This definition of engagement has important distinctions from others. Some equate engagement with time-on-task, but such a definition implies that more able, faster readers are less engaged than less able readers. For most scholars, engagement entails some kind of mindfulness, cognitive effort and deep processing of new information. Another view equates engagement with intrinsic motivation. For Jacques, Preece, and Carey, "learners are 'engaged' with educational multimedia when it holds their attention and they are attracted to it for intrinsic rewards". Though intrinsic motivation may foster engagement, it does not differentiate attraction to superficial aspects of text and "mindful" involvement.

Simple conceptions of intrinsic motivation fail to address issues of volition, complex cognitive-affective-motivational acts that manage and implement goals in the fact of distractions. Some researchers equate engagement with self-regulated learning. However, self-regulated learning, planning, monitoring, and managing of one's own learning, is often a 'cold' construct, emphasizing metacognitive processes over meta-motivational and meta-affective aspects of personal meaning-making.

High literacy requires high engagement, the coordination of cognitive, affective, and motivational strategies. Substantive engagement requires sustained commitment to and engagement in the problems and issues of academic study. However, procedurally engaged students comply with minimal requirements for accomplishing school assignments, and disengaged students are off-task. Recipient learning reflected generally low strategy use. Resource management reflected high use of cognitive strategies to obtain but not transform information. Task-focused learning reflected high use of cognitive strategies to change but not acquire information.

Identifying student, software, and contextual interactions that promote high literacy would help us understand and enrich the interdependence of motivation and cognition in learning. But discussion of student engagement with computer software has only begun. Software content, software features, and learning task might influence student engagement with software. Student engagement with software will be reactive, proactive, or mutual, depending whether the software is tutorial, generative, or mutually adaptive.

REFERENCES

Ackermann, E., *Tools for Teaching: The World Wide Web and a Web Browser*, 1996.

Bichelmeyer, B. A., Kiggins, E.A., "Using Web-based Conferencing in Post-secondary Instruction", *Proceedings of the Annual Conference on Distance Teaching and Learning*, Madison, WI, August 5-7, 1998.

Brundage, D., Keane, R., and Mackneson, R., "Application of Learning Theory to the Instruction of Adults", In Thelma Barer-Stein and James A. Draper (eds.), *The Craft of Teaching Adults*, pp. 131-144. Toronto, Ontario: Culture Concepts, 1993.

Burge, E., "Adult Distance Learning: Challenges for Contemporary Practice". In Thelma Barer-Stein and James A. Draper (eds.), *The Craft of Teaching Adults,* pp.215-230, Toronto, Ontario: Culture Concepts, 1993.

Burow-Flake, E., Kocher, D., Reiser, A., *Changing Students, Changing Classroom Landscapes: Meeting the Challenge in the Small Liberal Arts Institution,* in L. Lloyd (ed.), *Teaching with Technology, Rethinking Tradition,* Medford, NJ: Information Today, Inc., 2000.

Forsyth, I., *Teaching and Learning Materials and the Internet* (2nd ed.), London: Kogan Page, 1998.

Jayanthi Ranjan, Sanjeevi Arul, "Online Teaching", *University News*, 38(3), January, 2001.

4
Multimedia Retrieval

The computer, television and the telephone have today converged into a single access digital technology, and such networks in turn are leading to a high speed reliable and robust data communication network systems. This convergence is enabling interactive, self-directed participation to obtain services, products and information. By virtue of this convergence, we can have interactive TV, video on demand running on our computer screens, mailboxes which convert voice to digital or text form and back again, desktop video conferencing and a variety of electronic devices such as newspapers, shopping malls and financial reports brought to us via public networks. Moreover, technology has migrated from analog (continuously variable signals) to digital (binary signals) steadily over the last two decades.

This trend has taken place not only in telecommunications, but in the computer industry as well. On the one hand, the analog copper wire based telephone network is gradually getting replaced and augmented with fibre optic-based digital technology, namely, the Integrated Service Digital Network (ISDN). On the other, fibre optic networks have the increased bandwidth and speed required to move large amounts of digitised data from one point to another via computer systems. The trend towards miniaturisation and the requirement for greater and greater storage capability was facilitated by the migration from floppy disc to read only memory compact disc (CD-ROM) which is capable of storing about a thousand times more data than a floppy disc and has become the medium of choice for distributing multimedia services.

In the beginnings, computers were developed to help military establishments in ballistic calculation, in military logistics and later in atomic physics. Computer technology was subsequently applied to research areas like computation of mathematical functions and resolving difficult problems in engineering. Commercial use of digital computers was first made by the aircraft industry and later by insurance companies.

Computers in higher education were first employed for research in applied mathematics, engineering science and astronomy during the 1950s. The 1960s saw computer-based methodology employed in the social sciences. The introduction of database technology in the 1970s, while extending its use to other disciplines, helped make computers more cost effective. Computer Aided Instruction (CAI) has been successfully applied to disciplines as varied as language and literature, biblical and religious studies, archaeology and history, as well as to teaching of ancient languages like Sanskrit, Greek, Latin, Egyptian and Sumerian.

Marshall Mcluhan rightly called the computer a prosthesis in the assistance of human intelligence. A remarkable modern tool, it is indeed a powerful aid in the field of mental endeavour. The ongoing shift from Gutenberg to new modes of communication has left its mark on the universities especially in humanities since they are text-centred studies and the culture of laboratories and computers is alien to them. That digital electronic transmission has become an important means of communication cannot be denied. Network systems today provide facilities for electronic mail, easy access to database, as well as opportunities for discussions and conference with colleagues from all over the world.

It would not come amiss therefore to familiarise oneself with some commonly used terms in electronic communication systems such as hypertext, document assembly, multimedia and software innovations.

i) *Hypertext systems*: The hypertext system link different parts of a work so that one can jump around the same work and also in and out of other work as the need arises. It opens up a world in which it is possible to work with books always present to one another and to us. We can acquire detailed information on one point, refer back to a previous document, compare with a third and then switch back to the main argument.

ii) *Document assembly*: The document assembly is a technique which enables work to be carried out in pre-determined formats like order forms, invoices, application forms, etc. All relevant forms are available on file and can be used as and when desired. Facts entered in the forms at one point may be used to fill in the forms automatically at any other point.

iii) *Multimedia*: The multimedia combines the use of diverse media. Thus a topic can be explored through text, video, music, graphics and other relevant modes. It can either be joined into one unit through use of hypertext or viewed sequentially.

iv) *Software innovations*: The software innovations allow for both hypertext systems and multimedia presentations viewing. Windows displays have been developed where screen can be enlarged or diminished to make room for others involving text or other media.

The advantages of digitalisation are demassification and interconnectivity:

i) *Demassification*: The entire contents of the *Oxford English Dictionary* can be conveniently stored on two thin CD-ROMs. Reading is not affected as the typeface can be limitlessly enlarged. It has furthermore been predicted that the ratio of data to matter will increase dramatically in the coming years.

ii) *Interconnectivity*: Storage of texts, images, sounds on electronic systems opens up unprecedented possibilities in higher education. Link ups with databases becomes possible throughout the country, and also internationally, thus leading to drastic cuts in inter-library loan expenditure.

In this digital age the key nomenclatures are being recast. Traditional definitions for traditional institutions like the book, the author, the editor, the publisher, the reader are undergoing rapid redefinition. Thus in the work centres of the National Library of France (Bibliotheque National de France) readers are being redefined in terms of the reading they practise (long term versus short term readers). Earlier categories of social (learned and popular), political (public and private) or economic (fee paying and non-fee paying) are no longer valid. The sundry problems which can be visualised in the process of digitalisation are:

i) *Unaccountability*: The printed book imposed limits to acquiring a text and modifying it; a costly book had to be shared or borrowed and it was considered unethical to cut up or mark someone else's copy. But with the advent of the electronic revolution all such considerations are passe. Writing no longer retains its fixity. Without fixity signification becomes uncertain. Books can be infinitely reduced and modified without any guarantee that the purity of a text will be maintained.

ii) *Control*: All control is removed from the hands of the originators of file contents. Interference is difficult to detect since it can occur at the speed of light without leaving behind any traces in the original document. An agreement therefore will have to be devised for the protection of copyright in a situation where virtually no control seems possible.

iii) *Monetary considerations*.

a) *Writers and publishers*: Publishers are motivated solely by the wish to make money. Authors need money but they also want recognition. A prerequisite of recognition is a wide readership. Thus begins a clash between authors who want a wider dissemination of text and publishers who do little to encourage use without payment building barriers to deny access.

b) *Users:* When a work is written primarily for information it needs to be used. Publishers claim that users must pay. Users do pay in the sense that they use the information received as starting points in their own work thus adding to the corpus of existing information.

iv) *Economic viability*: The single most important factor behind escalating prices of the book is the spiralling cost of paper. Due to the scarcity of trees paper has become expensive and printing on paper is now a costly venture. Digitalisation will usher in a paperless society but it will require substitute materials. Conversion of documents into electronic media will be an expensive exercise. Initial investment in installation of access services and infrastructure will be heavy. Conservation and maintenance cost will be high.

v) *Security systems*: Computer criminals, virus producers, saboteurs and hackers pose grave threats. Academic work is virtually accessible worldwide. No effective copyright laws exist. Banking systems, especially financial transactions, need to be protected. Access detection systems are still expensive.

vi) *Modes of textuality*: Digitalisation holds out the promise of a limitless expansion of knowledge and our ability to access it but it ushers in a new mode of textuality different from that of the printed text. Whereas the digital text is a matter of immediate and continuous apprehension the book is a more leisurely and slower form of expression. It is, as Marcel Proust has said, a fulcrum that creates space out of time. It gives us time to investigate, reflect and contemplate and is a rather slow and tedious path to knowledge and action.

vii) *Validity of human experience*: The necessity to preserve the validity of human experience becomes the duty of every human being. In the electronic world human experiences threaten to be reduced to the status of a pure memory flow of an online exchange.

Multimedia computer uses the normal output media of display screen, printed hard copy alongwith recorded high quality audio, high quality still images, animation or recorded motion video. The words recorded and high quality should not be overlooked—they refer to the capability of the multimedia computer to successfully display images, video or sound that has been captured from live sources, much like the capability of a television system.

Capturing from live sources is in addition to the computer's inherent ability to generate its own pictures or sounds through software, which we refer to as simulation. This emphasis on real or natural sounds and pictures is important for it greatly enhances the realism of a computer presentation; it tremendously expands the sources of materials that we can display or present within a computer.

Now, in addition to signing our name on a document, we can use our own photograph or our own voice to sign. If we want to show a real object as part of our presentation, we can simply point a video camera at it and click a button to include that in our work.

Modern network capability has grown to the point where distributing multimedia via a digital network is now practical. IBM has articulated a concept, which they call enterprise multimedia, where every PC or workstation in an organisation is multimedia ready and the network and its servers can handle multimedia traffic along with the other data. Multimedia objects can be stored at any server and made available to users of the network on demand. The enterprise multimedia concept depends on the use of all-digital multimedia.

A hybrid analog digital system will not work with the digital network. An important possibility, once corporate-wide digital networks are in place, is to use the network for tele-conferencing. Each participant remains in his own office, but by means of a digital audio connection through the network, he can communicate with the other participants, regardless of where they are located. Using the other multimedia data types, such as video, graphics, images or animation, any participant can introduce illustrative material into the meeting to facilitate better communication.

The ISDN is valuable for multinational corporations using data communications to connect international small to medium branch office Local Area Networks (LANs). But ISDN is not just for internet-working LANs over the wide area; it can be used as a high speed, dial-up link to the internet and is well suited for the International Telecommunications Union (ITU)'s recently approved T.120 multimedia conference standards.

It even supports video-conferencing. Since ideas on what exactly constitutes a multimedia presentation vary, the standard allows equipment to support subsets of the specification. For example, two video tele-conferencing units sharing a conference with devices that support only audio and still image, or audio only, must be able to work together at the most basic level of voice communication. The premise behind a multimedia tele-conference is similar to video, in that groups can communicate effectively while avoiding the cost and time lost in travel. The emerging applications of multimedia are the following:

1) *Training or education application*: The multimedia computer really shines when used for training or education in a one-to-one situation with a student. The multimedia presentation capability can show the student,

material from any kind of source text, charts, audio, video, animations, simulations or photographs. When these are combined with interactivity, an effective learning environment is created. Multimedia training is also extremely effective in teaching someone how to use a computer programme and many recent releases of productivity and multimedia programmes include multimedia tutorials.

2) *Information delivery applications*: Many multimedia applications exist in order to give a user access to some class of data. Vast collection of data are in the form of books, catalogues, libraries, audio tapes, video tapes or still photographs. Any of these can be captured in digital format and presented by a multimedia computer; this is called information delivery and the other application is the CDROM disc.

3) *Merchandising applications*: Selling combines information delivery with other capabilities such as demonstration, quotation, negotiation, order taking and so on. The information delivery capability is an excellent front end for a programme that sells products. Authoring for sales applications is usually done by programming in an authoring language.

4) *Productivity applications*: Productivity applications such as spread-sheets, charting programmes or database programmes create screens that are displayed to show the user's data or calculations. It is valuable if the user can add multimedia objects to these screens so that he can use audio or video to support or explain his screens.

5) *Tele-conferencing*: The technologies of digital networks and multimedia promise to alleviate many of these problems through what is called tele-conferencing. With this, one can participate in a meeting without leaving his desk or workstation and he can still obtain the kind of audiovisual experience he would get by travelling to a live meeting.

6) *Geographic information systems*: Management of facilities such as buildings, roads, power lines and railroad tracks is a problem that concerns government offices, utilities and many industries. Specially designed computer database management systems called geographic information systems are available to provide online support for these types of applications.

Multimedia enables a single user to interact with several applications; previously it was not possible to provide viewing and interactive capability to a number of users simultaneously and on demand. Multimedia networking has provided the ability to dispense information to a wide audience—in office, school or home—in order to entertain, inform and train a large number of people in a uniform and consistent manner. In order to meet such objective, researchers have addressed issues such as speed and bandwidth of network server capabilities, capital investment in multimedia PCs, access to information systems and databases, custom-developed applications, cross-platform delivery and interactive as well as store-and-forward multimedia systems. The major features of a multimedia system are the following:

i) The major front end of a multimedia is the audio which comprises an audio adapter, an audio input device such as a microphone, software to digitise the analog sound, amplifiers and speakers.

ii) Rapid advances in video digitisation technology have enabled video to be harnessed and deployed on the desktop. Real-time video delivery, that is, delivering the presentation live requires a high-speed, high-bandwidth network.

iii) Video-conferencing is another real-time video application. A video-conference can be point-to-point between two locations or multipoint, which can include several conference sites, depending on the system's capabilities. In several situations, real-time video delivery may not be necessary. In such cases a store-and-forward technology is adopted, in which a user can access a library of video presentations from his multimedia computer. The bandwidth and network speed requirements are proportionately lower.

iv) Animation is another feature of multimedia capabilities. Two-dimensional (2D) animation is the most common type today, such as cartoons. However, 3D animation has mostly been confined to the engineering field like in computer-aided design (CAD). As 3D animation technology matures and becomes more competitive, this feature will also get into applications like online tutorials, simulations and virtual reality.

v) The Virtual Reality (VR) applications are programmes that could envelop a user within a 3D simulated environment of sight, movement, sound and possibly touch in the future.

There are four types of multimedia computer systems:

i) A multimedia application is best created on a developer workstation and viewed on an end user computer system deploying digital video capturing devices, minicomputer and studio sound system.

ii) The multimedia on a desktop would be a low-end system suitable for viewing and interacting with multimedia applications called an MPC level 2 machine running at 25 MHz with at least 4 MB of RAM.

iii) A multimedia kiosk system would be a computer system generally located in high-traffic area such as railway station, airport, restaurant or office. A viewer can interact with the system via computer running a multimedia application. Portable multimedia systems have been made possible through the revolution in wireless technology.

iv) Portable computer systems such as laptops, palmtops and personal digital assistants (PDAs) are becoming smaller and lighter in weight, yet possessing considerable processing power, speed and storage capacity.

The most important issues of multimedia are: standardisation, privacy, and security.

i) *Standardisation*: In order to enable fully flexible development, distribution and widespread deployment of multimedia applications, the most serious problem is the absence of a common international vendor independent standards.
ii) *Privacy issues*: The need for privacy requires that a user should be secure or protected from electronic access, intrusion and surveillance and still be able to interact with the system. It is also necessary that developers should take care not to invade in any way the privacy of people whose names, likeness and images appear in an application.
iii) *Security issues*: All electronic information is vulnerable to encroachment in some form or the other and organisations must prevent unauthorised access. Intentional or unintended abuse and accidental destruction of data can prove extremely harmful to the service provider. To gain access, the relevant staff must have the proper authorisation to view and interact with the application.

The major applications of multimedia include:

i) *Video on demand*: Video on demand is a user friendly method of providing video programming. The viewer decides when the programme will begin and not the TV company. The selected programme is instantly delivered to the user, right from the beginning. If someone chooses the same title a second later, it is delivered to that person also from the beginning. The same multimedia title can be viewed by any number of people concurrently, with each individual choosing his own viewing time.

ii) *Entertainment*: Multimedia networking is probably used most of all in the entertainment industry, where applications are almost unlimited.

iii) *Interactive television*: The Interactive Television (ITV) overcomes the drudgery of simply viewing the tube.

iv) *Medicine*: Information about a patient such as X-ray, magnetic resonance imaging (MRI) scan, photographs, laboratory reports, case histories can be digitised and transmitted to the doctor anywhere anytime.

v) *Manufacturing*: Multimedia is growing more and more popular in this industry day by day. Touch-screen workstations assist the technician on the assembly line or in the production process and his queries can be answered by the system on touch screen by online video instructions.

vi) *Retail business*: Many retail outlets are using multimedia computers as sales tools. The customer can have the product shown in a variety of colours and from which the buyer can see the preview of the play, the concert or the game from his chosen seat before actually making the purchase.

In a developing country like India, digitalisation is still a fanciful unreality for the majority. Equipment is still too expensive, software scarce and power supplies, irregular. Lack of spare parts and components often makes it easier to replace than to repair.

The ERNET, a computer networking project, set up as a joint venture between the United Nations Development Programme and the Department of Electronics in 1986, is still beyond the reach of the masses. The total number of computers in India is comparatively small. Government statistics claim that there is one computer per thousand in this country.

CONTENT-BASED VISUAL INFORMATION RETRIEVAL (CBVIR) SYSTEMS

To overcome the limitations of text-based retrieval, researchers started to investigate possible ways of retrieving multimedia information—particularly images and video clips—based solely on its contents. Instead of being manually annotated using keywords, images and video clips would be indexed by their own visual content, such as colour, texture, objects' shape and movement, among others. Research in the field of Content-Based Visual Information Retrieval (CBVIR) started in the early 1990's and is likely to continue during the next decade. Design of CBVIR systems brings up many interesting problems and challenges. An important subset of these problems is related to the way human beings perceive visual information and how much the knowledge of the human visual perception can help translating it into a set of features, rules, and criteria for comparing and selecting images. An example of a problem that falls into this category is the understanding of how human being, express their (subjective) understanding of the contents of an image using words, drawings, sketches, or similar images. A closely related problem is to understand how human beings perceive visual similarities. These and other similar problems have a great impact on the design of contemporary CBVIR systems.

The main blocks of a generic CBVIR system include:

i) User interface
ii) Query/search engine
iii) Digital image and video archive
iv) Visual summaries
v) Indexes
vi) Digitisation and compression and
vii) Cataloguing.

CBVIR systems typically rely on minimum amount of metadata or none at all. Digitisation, compression, and cataloguing typically happen off-line. Once these three steps have been performed, the database contains the images and videos themselves, possible simplified representations of each file or segment, and a collection of indexes that act as pointers to the corresponding images or video segments.

User interface is a most important component of a CBVIR system. Such interface should provide integrated browsing, viewing, searching, and querying capabilities in a clear and intuitive way. This integration is extremely important, since it is very likely that the user will not always stick to the best match found by the query/search engine. More often than not the user will want to check the first few best matches, browse through them. Searching the visual database contents should be made possible in several different ways either alone or combined. An ideal CBVIR system query stage would hide the technical complexity of the query process from the end user.

The systems should be able to automatically extract visual features that are used to describe the contents of an image or video clip. Examples of such features include colour, texture, size, shape, and motion information. The process of feature extraction can be enhanced and/or adapted to detect other, specialised attributes, such as human faces or objects. Because of perception subjectivity, there is no best representation for a given feature. The colour information, for instance, can be represented using different colour models and mathematical constructs, such as colour histograms, colour moments, colour sets, colour coherence vectors, or colour correlograms.

Users perception of visual contents is strongly associated to high-level, semantic information about the scene. Current Computer Vision techniques work at a lower level. Generally the user is looking for higher-level semantic features of the desired image, such as "a beautiful rose garden", "a batter hitting a baseball", or "an expensive sports car". There is no easy or direct mapping between the low-level features and the high-level concepts. The distance between these two worlds is normally known as "semantic gap."

There are basically two ways of minimising the semantic gap. The first consists of adding as much metadata as possible to the images, which was already discussed and shown to be impractical. The second suggests the use of rich user interaction with relevance feedback combined with learning algorithms to make the system understand and learn the semantic context of a query operation.

In the field of CBVIR, current Computer Vision and Image Processing techniques would be enough for image search and retrieval. The modest success rates experienced by such systems encouraged researchers to try a different approach, emphasising interactivity and explicitly including the human user in the loop.

The relevance feedback is the process by which a system gathers information from its users about the relevance of features, images, image regions, or partial retrieval results obtained so far. Such feedback might be provided in many different ways and each system might use it in a particular manner to improve its performance. The effect of relevance feedback is to move the query in the direction of relevant images and away from the non-relevant ones.

Relevance feedback has been used in contemporary CBVIR systems, such as MIT's FourEyes, UIUC's MARS, and NEC's PicHunter, among many others. In CBVIR systems that support relevance feedback a search typically consists of a query followed by repeated user feedback, where the user comments on the items that were retrieved.

The use of relevance feedback makes the user interactions with the system simpler and more natural. There are many ways of using the information provided by the user interactions and refining the subsequent retrieval results of a CBVIR system. One approach concentrates on the query phase and attempts to use the information provided by relevance feedback to refine the queries. Another option is to use relevance feedback information to modify feature weights, such as in the MARS project. A third idea is to use relevance feedback to construct new features or the fly, as exemplified by. A fourth possibility is to use the relevance feedback information to update the probability of each image in a database being the target image, in other words, to predict the goal image given the user's interactions with the system.

Designing a CBVIR system accessible through the internet extends its usefulness to users anywhere in the world at the expense of new design constraints. Numerous CBVIR systems, both commercial and research, have been developed in recent years. Most systems support random browsing; query by example; query by sketch; text-based query and navigation with customised categories. Systematic studies involving actual users in practical applications still need to be done to explore the tradeoffs among the different options.

Some of the currently available CBVIR systems are:

i) *Query By Image Content (QBIC)*: QBIC was the first commercial CBVIR system. It was developed by IBM Almaden Research Centre. Its framework and techniques have influenced many later systems. QBIC supports queries based on example images, user-constructed sketches, and selected colours and texture patterns. In its most recent version, it allows text-based keyword search to be combined with content-based similarity search.

ii) *Photobook:* It is a set of interactive tools for browsing and searching images developed at MIT Media Lab. Photobook consists of three sub-books, from which shape, texture, and face features are extracted respectively. Users can query the system based on features from each of the three sub-blocks.

iii) *FourEyes:* It is an improved version of Photobook that includes user relevance feedback. Given a set of positive and negative examples, it decides upon which models or combinations of models to use and learns which combinations work best for solving particular types of problems. When presented with a new problem similar to one it has solved before, FourEyes can solve it more quickly than it could the first time.

iv) *Netra:* Netra is a prototype CBVIR system developed in the UCSB Alexandria Digital Library (ADL) project. It uses colour, shape, texture, and spatial location information in the segmented image regions to search and retrieve similar images from the database.

v) *Multimedia Analysis and Retrieval System (MARS)*: The main focus of MARS is not on finding a single "best" feature representation, but rather on how to organise the various visual features into a meaningful retrieval architecture, which can dynamically adapt to different applications and different users. MARS formally proposes a relevance feedback architecture in Image Retrieval and integrates such technique at various levels during retrieval, including query vector refinement, automatic matching tool selection, and automatic feature adaptation.

vi) *PicToSeek:* PicToSeek uses autonomous web crawlers to collect images on the web. Then, the collected images are automatically catalogued and classified into predefined classes and their relevant features are extracted. The users can query PicToSeek using image features, an example image, or simply browsing the precomputed image catalogue.

REFERENCES

Dede, C. J., "The Future of Multimedia: Bridging to Virtual Worlds, *Educational Technology*, 1992.

Dowe, J., "Content-based Retrieval in Multimedia Imaging", *Proc, SPIE Conference on Storage and Retrieval fro Image and Video Databases*, 1993.

Flikner, M., Sawhney H., Niblack W., Ashley J., Huang, Q., Dom, B., Gorkani, M., Hafner J., Lee, D., Petkovic D., Steele D., Yanker

P., "Query by Image and Video Content: The QBIC System", in *Intelligent Multimedia Information Retrieval*, Maybury, M.T., (ed.)., American Association for Artificial Intelligence (AAAI), Melno Park, CA, 1997.

Gevers. T., Smeulders, W.M., "The PicToSeek WWW Image Search System", *Proceedings of the International Conference on Multimedia Computing and Systems*, Florence, Italy, 1999.

Li. W., "Integrating Image Matching and Classification fro Multimedia Retreival on Web", *Proceedings of the International Conference on Multimedia Computing Systems*, Florence, Italy, 1999.

Marques O., Furht B., "Issues in Designing Contemporary Video Database Systems", *Proc. IASTED Conference on Internet and Multimedia Systems and Applications,* Nassau, Bahamas, October, 1999.

Mukherea S., Hirata K., Hara Y., "Towards a Multimedia World Wide Web", *Information Retrieval Engine*, http://www.decweb.ethz.ch/.

Pentland A., Picard R.W., Sclaroff S., "Photobook: Content-based Manipulation of Image Databases", Chapter 2, *Mutimedia Tools and Applications*, Furht, B.Ed., Kluwer Academic Publishers, Boston, 1996.

Stuart, R. and Thomas, J. C., "The Implications of Education in Cyberspace", *Multimedia Review*, 1991.

Rui. Y., Huang, T.S., S. Mehrotra and Ortega M., *A Relevance Feedback Architecture for Content-based Multimedia Information Systems*, 1997.

Wilson, A., "Instructional Multimedia in the Math Classroom and Beyond", *Paper presented at the Annual Conference of the American Mathematical Association of Two-year Colleges*, Tulsa, OK, November 3-6, 1994.

5

Instructional Technology and Virtual Space

The pace of both technological development and their introduction of new technologies into educational settings has dramatically accelerated during the past few decade. Throughout the 1970s and 1980s, technical innovation brought increasingly diverse and more powerful technological tools into schools. These technologies were typically text-based, locally networked or stand-alone computer-assisted instruction applications. The combination of computation, connectivity, visual and multimedia capacities, and speed have radically changed the potential for technologies in schooling. These developments are now making it possible for technologies to be designed and deployed to produce powerful and linked technologies that can substantially address some of the core problems of education.

Instructional development is an essential process in distance education, where the instructor and students may share limited common background and typically have minimal face-to-face contact. The instructional development process is taking place in the following stages:

i) design stage;
ii) development stage;
iii) evaluation stage; and
iv) revision stage.

Design stage: The design stage begins with the process of determining the need for instruction by considering what external data verify the need, what factors led to the instructional need, and what past experiences indicate that the instruction being planned can effectively meet this need. To better understand the distant learners and their needs, consider their ages, cultural backgrounds, past experiences, interests and educational levels. When possible, the instructor should visit distant sites and interview prospective students, both individually and in small groups. This personalised attention will also show students that the instructor is more than an anonymous presence, linked by electronic technology. Based on the nature of the problem as well as student needs and characteristics, establish instructional goals.

Development stage: The instructor should create an outline of the content to be covered, based on the instructional problems, instructional goals, and an understanding of the desired course content. Instructional materials should not be used solely because they are readily available or have been effective in a traditional classroom setting. This is especially true if prepackaged materials, such as telecourses, are being considered.

Whereas many pre-packaged instructional tools are developed and marketed to reach students with similar backgrounds and experiences, they may have little relevance for distant learners who come to the course with widely varied and non-traditional experiential backgrounds. If pre-packaged materials are to be used, consider developing wrap around introductions, conclusions, and summaries that specifically relate the learning materials to the instructional context of the distant student.

Development of instructional materials and selection of delivery methods will often require integrating print, voice, video, and data technology in concert with face-to-face communication. The challenge here is to integrate delivery components, based on identifiable learner needs, content requirements, and technical constraints.

Evaluation stage: The main aim of evaluation is to determine if the instructional methods and materials are accomplishing the established goals and objectives. Implementation of instruction represents the first real test of what has been developed. Try to pre-test instruction on a small scale prior to implementation. If this is not possible, the first actual use will also serve as the field test for determining effectiveness. Plan how and when to evaluate the effectiveness of the instruction. Formative evaluation can be used to revise instruction as the course is being developed and implemented. For example, the distance educator can give students pre-addressed and stamped postcards to complete and mail after each session. These "mini-evaluations" might focus on course strengths and weaknesses, technical or delivery concerns, and content areas in need of further coverage. Summative evaluation is conducted after instruction is completed and provides a data base for course revision and future planning. Following course completion, consider a summative evaluation session in which students informally brainstorm ways to improve the course. Consider having a local facilitator run the evaluation session to encourage a more open discussion. Within the context of formative and summative evaluation, data are collected through quantitative and qualitative methods.

Quantitative evaluation relies on a breadth of response and is patterned after experimental research focused on the collection and manipulation of statistically relevant quantities of data. In contrast, qualitative evaluation focuses on a depth of response, using more subjective methods such as interviews and observation to query a smaller number of respondents in greater depth. Qualitative approaches may be of special value because the diversity of distant learners may defy relevant statistical stratification and analysis. The best approach often combines quantitative measurement of student performance with open-ended interviewing and non-participant observation to collect and assess information about attitudes toward the course's effectiveness and the delivery technology.

Revision stage: Revision plans typically are a direct result of the evaluation process in tandem with feedback from colleagues and content specialists. The best source of revision ideas may be the instructor's own reflection on course strengths and weaknesses. For this reason, revision should be planned as soon as possible after course completion. Often, course revisions will be minor, such as breaking a large and unwieldy instructional unit into more manageable components, increasing assignment feedback, or improving student-to-student interaction. On other occasions, major revisions will be needed. Significant course changes should be field-tested prior to future course use. Test revision ideas on small groups of distant learners, content specialists, and colleagues. Results of this process should be tempered by the knowledge that the characteristics of each distant class will vary and that revisions required for one learner group may be inappropriate for a different student population. While it is possible, even appropriate on occasion, to shorten the instructional development process, it should be done only after considering the needs of the learner, the requirements of the content, and the constraints facing both teacher and students.

INSTRUCTIONAL MEDIA

Media is a kind of message of delivery system which includes all kinds of mechanical devices directed to educational use. These devices are used as means of communicating our ideas to large number of people who are located in far off areas. Choice of media is crucial where there is no provision for face-to-face interaction and the students depend on print material with occasional face-to-face support. Distance education programmes can be enriched and made more attractive, effective and satisfying by using a variety of media relevant to the content for learning and the facilities that can be provided should attempt an exploitation of the potential of the variety of powerful media provided by modern technology. The educational media was confined to classroom lectures supported by print material. Education was imparted with the help of maps, charts, pictures, books, diagrams and till recently through using 11 mm projectors for educational purposes. Actually the 1970's were the decade of print.

The present day mechanical devices have brought about a virtual revolution in diverse field of human activity. A variety of media are used in distance education in open universities as well as in institutes of distance learning. They can be classified into two groups:

i) print media and
ii) non-print media.

Education system cannot do anything without printed course material. It is the mainstay of the instructional system almost everywhere. It is in the form of reading material or in the form of programmed instructional material. It is the most popular medium because it is easy to carry, is comparatively cheaper and can be used according to the convenience of the learners. The learners get the self- instructional material at their homes by post. The material is carefully prepared by experts in the field of their expertise to suit the needs of the learners and to help them learn the subject without much assistance from others.

The non-print media includes the technologies such as radio and television, telephone, videotex, computers, internet, satellites and so on.

Print media

Education system cannot do anything without printed course material. It is the mainstay of the instructional system almost everywhere. It is in the form of reading material or in the form of programmed instructional material. It is the most popular medium because it is easy to carry, is comparatively cheaper and can be used according to the convenience of the learners.

The learners get the self- instructional material at their homes by post. The material is carefully prepared by experts in the field of their expertise to suit the needs of the learners and to help them learn the subject without much assistance from others.

Non-print Media

Radio

Radio has become one of the most powerful media of mass communication in the modern age. It is being increasingly used in advanced countries to overcome the shortage of qualified teachers and suitable books. It can enrich the farthest corners. If the radio has become a necessary instrument of education in advanced and progressive countries, the services it can render are still far greater in a country like India. As a matter of fact, the radio is an effective medium and has been extensively used for educational purposes to spread literacy or to give formal or non-formal education all over the world. In addition to the printed materials lessons are planned and written for broadcast from All India Radio.

Radio programmes supplement and reinforce instruction imparted through the printed material. The radio is within the reach of the common man and can be carried along from place to place.

Television

Television is a more effective medium than radio for spreading education, because the language of TV is rich, powerful and expressive. TV lessons are entertaining as well as attractive. A lesson received through the gates of eyes and ears has a double chance of retention by learners. The television screen may become the electronic blackboard of the future. Radio and television are not teacher substitute but teaching aids only. They are very useful, produce more elaborate illustrative material, have tremendous potential but they cannot stand on their own. In India also the majority of the students of distance education have started making use of TV for educational purposes. The UGC programmes are becoming very popular these days.

Instructional television (ITV)

Instructional television (ITV), is an effective distance education delivery system that can be integrated into the curriculum at three basic levels:

i) *Single lesson*: Programs address one specific topic or concept, providing a lesson introduction, overview, or summary.

ii) *Selected unit*: A series of programmes providing the content foundation for a learning unit in the course curriculum.

iii) *Full course*: Programs from one or more ITV series may be integrated into a full semester course typically in conjunction with instructional print materials.

There are two types of ITV—passive or interactive. Passive ITV typically involves pre-produced programmes which are distributed by video cassette or by video-based technologies such as broadcast, cable, or satellite. In contrast, interactive ITV provides opportunities for viewer interaction, either with a live instructor or a participating student site. For example, two-way television with two-way audio allows all students to view and interact with the teacher. At the same time, cameras at remote sites allow the teacher to view all participating students. It is also possible to configure the system so that all student sites may view one another.

Taking advantage of the visual imagery of ITV can counter an over-reliance on lecturing. Carefully planning ways to show instead of tell may improve the instructional effectiveness of ITV. It may be helpful to visually represent:

i) Outlines or lists
ii) Key points
iii) Complex material in a step-by-step fashion
iv) Relationships
v) Information that needs to be summarised for retention and recall.

The teachers should make use of:

i) *Pictures:* To show what things look like.
ii) *Diagrams*: To illustrate conceptual relationships, organisations, and structure of content material.
iii) *Maps*: To show spatial relationships.
iv) *Graphs, tables, and charts:* To summarise information.

Take advantage of video's ability to show movement to:

i) Demonstrate the operation of tools and equipment.
ii) Demonstrate skills that learners are expected to emulate.
iii) Conduct experiments in which the processes must be observed.
iv) Analyse change over time using animation, slow motion, or time lapse photography.
v) Reveal the spatial, three-dimensional qualities of an object or structure.
vi) Transport learners to places or situations not otherwise in their experience.
vii) Present primary source materials for analysis, such as film of historical events or naturally occurring situations.

The teacher's real challenge is to psychologically reduce the gap not only through the appropriate use of technology but also through the use of effective teaching practices. Good teaching ensures that a rapport develops between students and teacher.

Once basic teaching methods are considered, try employing the following three step strategy for conducting ITV lessons:

i) *Set the stage*

a) Remember that it takes longer to deliver instruction at a distance than in a traditional face-to-face setting. Plan lessons accordingly.

b) Practice in front of a live camera prior to class. If possible, have a colleague, a few target students, or a media technician view your presentation and on-camera presence, offering suggestions for improvement.

c) Organise all class materials and visuals before the start of the class. It is best to have a trial run with technical staff so that all participants know the role they are expected to play.

d) If using an overhead camera to electronically project visuals, understand its operation and limitations prior to the start of the class.

e) Prepare viewers for new terminology to be used in the programme, and answer any questions regarding the technical equipment being used, such as cameras, television monitors, audio equipment, etc..

f) Inform students if there will be camera operators or technicians in the classroom. Although the students may be initially curious, this will fade as the class progresses. In-class technicians are trained to be as unobtrusive as possible.

g) Students should have the necessary background materials to make the best use of televised lessons. Consider the use of study questions to assist in focusing discussions.

h) Consider team teaching to maintain viewer interest with a change of voice, image, and presentation style. If using guest speakers, give students necessary background information prior to the class. Do the same for the guest speakers. Let them know the specific purpose of their session, what is expected of them, and the general background of participating students.

ii) *During the ITV session*

a) Vary facial expressions, tone of voice, body movements, and eye contact with the camera to enhance verbal communication.

b) Engage students by using humour, asking questions, involving students, and praising student contributions.

c) Maintain energy and dynamism to attract and hold the distant learners' attention. Remember, enthusiasm is contagious. So is boredom.

d) Present content in five to ten minute blocks interspersed with discussion. Alternate between instruction and interaction.

e) Keep lecture sessions simple and clear. To help focus viewing, indicate key points to look for.

f) Do not read material.

g) Maintain a moderate speaking pace.

h) Do not digress—keep students on track.

i) Include different kinds of student involvement—watching, reading, writing, and talking.

j) Vary the centre of focus for activities from the on-camera presenter to a receive site group or individual.

k) Incorporate timely breaks as a respite from the television monitor.

l) Motivate peer learning and support by encouraging students to work together both in and out of class.

m) Review the concepts discussed in the programme and clarify any misunderstandings by asking focused questions.

n) Integrate activities to reinforce the content presentation. These activities might include quizzes, worksheets, role-playing, and experiments.

o) Make sure opportunities are included to enhance student interaction by:

— Planning a block of time for interaction and then letting students know in advance that interaction is anticipated. Initiating an interaction within the first twenty minutes will get students motivated to participate in learning rather than lulling them into just watching.

— Designating students at distant sites to lead discussions or survey the room for questions.

— Clearly defining discussion topics or questions and then allowing time for students to prepare responses. Assigning discussion questions in advance of the television session will help students prepare for the interaction. Have the questions appear in writing on the screen so students see and hear the questions.

— Encouraging student-to-student interaction by asking an in-class student or a student from a distant site to respond to questions. The instructor does not always have to answer questions.

— Functioning as content facilitator not just content provider.

iii) *Following the session*

a) Review the taped recordings of the presentation, either with technical staff, a colleague, or by yourself. Take notes for improving presentation, style, and delivery methods.

b) Seek student feedback on the strengths and weaknesses of the instructional materials and the teaching strategies being used.

c) Be open to new ideas and delivery techniques for improving instructional effectiveness.

Since most people have watched television, the medium is familiar. Motion and visuals can be combined in a single format so that complex or abstract concepts can be illustrated through visual simulation. The old cliche a picture is worth a thousand words rings true. Instructional television is an effective way to take students to new environments. Time and space can be collapsed, so that events can be captured and relayed as they happen. It is very effective for introducing, summarising, and reviewing concepts.

As any other medium Instructional Television has its own limitations The Broadcast quality ITV is expensive to create. Video production is time consuming and can be technically demanding, often requiring relatively sophisticated production facilities and equipment. Sites choosing to interactively participate in an ITV programme may require specialised equipment, facilities, and staffing. Most prepackaged ITV courses use a mass media approach to instruction aimed at the average student. As a result, they can be ineffective in serving students with special needs. When used passively, without interaction, its instructional effectiveness can be limited. Unless professionally produced, completed ITV programmes often look amateurish. Once completed, ITV programmes can be difficult to revise and update.

Audio/video cassettes

Audio/video cassettes can be played and replayed at home by the learner at his/her will. A learner can stop a particular tape at a point where more details are necessary and can play in slow motion to understand a difficult point. He need not get up early in the morning or wake up late in the night for radio and TV broadcasts. The use of video enabled a good lecturer to be seen and heard all over the country, without having to repeat his performance. At the moment, the video equipment is costly in India and even in other developing countries and they are not within the reach of most of the students.

Telephone

Telephone is a very effective means of communication. It offers two ways interactive communications across distance, i.e., people can talk to each other, discuss and ask questions. In India this is unlikely to be considered as a medium in distance education.

Videotex

The videotex makes home television sets to function like a computer terminal and retrieve text information and graphics from a remote database. It gives much wider access to information and much wider ease with which new concepts and ideas can be transmitted.

Computers

The rapid development of computer networks, dramatic improvements in the processing power of personal computers, and striking advances in magnetic storage technology have made the computer a dynamic force in distance education, providing a new and interactive means of overcoming time and distance to reach learners. Computer applications for distance education fall into four broad categories:

i) *Computer-assisted Instruction (CAI)*: Uses the computer as a self-contained teaching machine to present discrete lessons to achieve specific but limited educational objectives. There are several CAI modes, including: drill and practice, tutorial, simulations and games, and problem-solving.

ii) *Computer-managed Instruction (CMI)*: Uses the computer's branching, storage, and retrieval capabilities to organise instruction and track student records and progress. The instruction need not be delivered via computer, although often CAI is combined with CMI.

iii) *Computer-mediated Communication (CMC)*: Describes computer applications that facilitate communication. Examples include electronic mail, computer conferencing, and electronic bulletin boards.

iv) *Computer-based Multimedia*: The goal of computer-based multimedia is to integrate various voice, video, and computer technologies into a single, easily accessible delivery system. HyperCard, hypermedia, and a still-developing generation of powerful, sophisticated, and flexible computing tools have gained the attention of distance educators in recent years.

In the CAI mode, computers individualise learning, while giving immediate reinforcement and feedback. With integrated graphic, print, audio, and video capabilities, computers can effectively link various technologies. Interactive video and CD-ROM technologies can be incorporated into computer-based instructional units, lessons, and learning environments. Microcomputer systems incorporating various software packages are extremely flexible and maximise learner control. By understanding their present needs and future technical requirements, the cost-conscious educator can effectively navigate the volatile computer hardware and software market. Local, regional, and national networks link resources and individuals, wherever they might be.

Although individual computers are relatively inexpensive and the computer hardware and software market is very competitive, it is still costly to develop instructional networks and purchase the system software to run them. Computer technology evolves so quickly that the distant educator focused solely on innovation "not meeting tangible needs" will constantly change equipment in an effort to keep pace with the "latest" technical advancements. Students must be highly motivated and proficient in computer operation before they can successfully function in a computer-based distance learning environment.

Internet

The internet is the largest, most powerful computer network in the world. It encompasses 1.3 million computers with internet addresses that are used up by 30 million people in more than fifty countries. As more colleges, universities, schools, companies and private citizens are connected to the internet either through affiliations with regional not-for-profit network or by subscribing to information services provided for profit companies, more possibilities are open for distance educators to overcome time and distance to reach students. The easy availability of computers and worldwide internet has brought about significant changes in learning-teaching strategies. In United States and Canada, every student has an e-mail account and has either a computer of his own or has easy access to the university computer system. This has solved to a great extent the problems of student and teacher interaction.

The present electronic communication system has made the interaction much easier and essentially less costly. With the access to internet, distance educators and their students can use the Electronic Mail (E-Mail), Bulletin Boards and World Wide Web (WWW). The WWW and web browsers have made the internet a more user-friendly environment.

The ability to integrate graphics, text, and sound into a single tool means that novice users do not have to struggle with such a steep learning curve. In addition, organisations and individuals can create home pages on their own computers or to pages created by others on different computer systems. In India, the UGC, the universities and the academic staff college can play an important role in bringing about this computer and internet revolution provided our college teachers and our research scholars are ready to use the new technologies to accelerate the pace of learning.

Education through web

In 1989, a group of scientists at the European Laboratory for Particle Physics (CERN) in Geneva, Switzerland began developing an internet tool that would link information produced by all of the CERN researchers. The tool provided a way to link textual information on different computers and created by different scientists. The object was to overcome issues of incompatibility and utilise a new way of linking made possible by computers, called hypertext. Rather than presenting information in a linear or hierarchical fashion, hypertext permits information to be linked in a web-like structure. Nodes of information can be linked to other nodes of information in multiple ways. As a result, users can dynamically criss-cross the information web using pieces in the order most convenient to them. The CERN project resulted in an innovative front-end to the internet, now referred to as the World-Wide Web (WWW). The WWW provides users with a uniform and convenient means of accessing the vast resources of the internet.

In 1993, the National Centre for Supercomputing Applications (NCSA) at the University of Illinois pushed the CERN scientists' idea further by creating a software tool called Mosaic. Mosaic is an easy to use graphical user interface that permits text, graphics, sound and video to be hyperlinked. Mosaic was the first of the internet tools that are now referred to as web browsers. Other well-known browsers include Netscape and Microsoft's Internet Explorer. Web browsers permit users to connect to the internet and facilitate accessing information located on another remote computer.

The web browser links to the remote computer just long enough so that the information you need can be sent to your computer for you to view. Documents created to be viewed by a browser are formatted using Hypertext Markup Language (HTML) HTML solves incompatibility problems by using standardised tags which indicate such things as whether a piece of text should be plain, bold, italic, or linked to another piece of text. Pages of information on a computer formatted with HTML and accessible to someone with a web browser, are referred to as home pages or web pages.

The WWW have made the internet a more user-friendly environment. The ability to integrate graphics, text, and sound into a single tool means that novice users do not have to struggle with such a steep learning curve. For educators, the WWW provides an exciting new opportunity for distance teaching and learning. The WWW can be used by the distance educator to build a classroom home page. The home page can cover information about the class including the syllabus, exercises, literature references, and instructor's biography. The instructor can also provide links to information on the WWW that would be useful to students in the class. Other links can access library catalogues or each student's individual home page.

Computer software tools such as HotMetal and HotDog mean that anyone familiar with using word processing software can develop a good looking and functional home page. Reviews of other such computer software tools are available on the WWW and many of them can be downloaded for a free trial. Utilise information that already has been developed for your course.

Hundreds of home pages have already been developed for courses. Some of these home pages allow students to complete an entire course from the WWW and others are developed in conjunction with lectures delivered on-campus or by video or audio.

To avoid ugly and confusing home pages, consider the following:

i) Consulting sites on the WWW which provide information on home page layout and style.
ii) Utilising a consistent format for each of your pages. Based on suggestions made by the above mentioned style manuals, develop a consistent format for each web page.

iii) Keeping page lengths short. Your main index should jump to a lot of shorter pages. In cases where page information is long, index internally so that the student can jump to specific information as needed.

iv) Maximising links to internal information and minimising links to external information.

v) Using unnecessarily large graphics or including sound/ video clips. Pages which take too long to download frustrate students and may force them to beat a hasty retreat. If your home page requires extensive use of graphics to demonstrate points, warn your students. If you plan to use sound or video clips, you will need to be sure that all of your distant students have access to computers that have sound and video cards installed in them.

v) Letting the home page become out-of-date. The home page should be an ongoing part of course development.

Properly designed home pages will encourage thought, discussion and active participation by your distant students. The following elements can be included in your class home page:

i) *Course and instructor information*: Include such items as course topics to be covered, your office hours, textbook information, course objectives, and grading policies.

ii) *Class communication*: Provide access to your e-mail, link to discussion groups that you have set up for student-to-student communication, and create forms that your students can use to report problems or provide biographical information about themselves.

iii) *Assignments and tests*: Distribute assignments and tests, provide for online completion or submission, and give solutions, hints, or samples of what you expect.

iv) *Material covered in the classroom*: Make lecture notes and handouts available either as web pages or as downloadable files.

v) *Demonstrations, animation, video, audio*: This is more complex than other suggestions and will require that your students have access to computers with sound and video cards.

vi) *Reference material*: List materials in print and electronic form that supplement the textbook.

Satellite

The satellite is the glamourous medium in distance education. It is used for communicating over long distance. More channels for both radio and television are possible because of the satellite. Programmes are viewed by people in cities as well as in countryside locations.

The satellite and television network offers a powerful medium for the dissemination of knowledge, cultural programme and developmental information. A wide area is covered without any loss of quality in the messages sent. The communication channels are not affected by natural calamities as is usually the case with telephone wires. All teaching and learning programmes can be greatly improved by visual and auditory materials because these make the learning experience far more concrete and memorable. But the media has remained under-exploited by the distance learning system for want of appropriate and relevant software which is the greatest problem of this system. India is making a mark in distance education and we need to develop and grow a large number of efficient, committed and trained media persons to implement new technologies in this field.

Interactive videoconferencing

Interactive Videoconferencing (IV) system can be integrated into the distance education programme with minimal adaptation to the curriculum and course and is designed to support two-way video and audio communication between multiple locations. Most IV systems utilise compressed digital video for the transmission of motion images over data networks such as high capacity Integrated Services Digital Networks (ISDN). The video compression process decreases the amount of data transmitted over the lines by transmitting only the changes in the picture. By minimising the bandwidth required to transmit the images, video compression also reduces the transmission cost. Interactive videoconferences are often transmitted on dedicated T-1 phone lines. These high speed lines are very effective for videoconferencing, but they are typically leased circuits with an expensive monthly cost. The fixed monthly charge is usually based on distance, not usage. Therefore, the cost effectiveness of IV systems increases with use.

Interactive videoconferencing systems can operate at different data rates, at various fractions of T-1 capacity, enabling the transmission of multiple simultaneous videoconferences over the same T-1 circuit. An IV system can also share a T-1 circuit with other digital data uses such as internet transmissions or file transfers. The core of IV is the codec (coder/decoder). This is the electronic device that transmits and receives the video signals that the class members will see on their television monitors. It may be easier to think of the codec as an extremely sophisticated modem. A modem takes digital data and transmits it over regular phone lines. The codec takes analog signals, compresses and digitises them, and transmits the signals over digital phone lines. Other types of equipment, such as television monitors, are needed to make IV successful.

Various forms of instructional technology can be incorporated into IV, including video cassette recorders/ players, microphones, cameras, and computers. Some systems are also capable of simultaneously connecting more than two sites through the use of a multi-point control unit, or MCU. Multi-point conferencing can be effective although the scheduling, technical, and logistical dimensions of MCU conferences can be imposing. A relatively new dial out feature, allows the use of multiple telephone lines to connect two or more sites in the same conference.

The three main types of videoconferencing systems existing today are:

i) *Small room videoconferencing*: This system is designed primarily for small groups at all sites seated around a conference table.
ii) *Classroom videoconferencing*: This type of system usually uses high quality AV components, codecs, and an interface that allows all participants to be seen on the monitors.
iii) *Desktop videoconferencing*: This system utilises a personal computer and videoconferencing software. These systems are less expensive, but offer limited resolution.

The IV lessons should incorporate a variety of activities for all students at the various sites. Use small group activities, student presentations, and an occasional break to add variety to the lesson. As a rule of thumb, instructors should change instruction methods every 10-15 minutes. It is often helpful to bring guest lecturers into the classroom. It may also be helpful to have guest speakers at one or more of the distant sites. When preparing class visuals, keep in mind that small fonts and light colours do not show up well over the monitors. A variety of formatting will also assist in maintaining student interest and attention. When formatting visuals, be sure that they will fit on the television monitor.

In the distance education classroom, the instructor should begin the course by preparing the learners for an active experience. Interactive videoconferencing is interactive, unlike regular television, and students can make the class much more interesting by being actively involved. By asking questions and noting body language, instructors can ascertain the interest and comprehension of the students at both all sites. This kind of attention will make all students feel more comfortable. An instructor be taught how to use all features of the equipment.

REFERENCES

Anderson, A H, Newlands, A, Mullin, J, Heming, A. M., Doherty-Sneddon, G and Van der Velden, J., "Impact of Video-mediated Communication on Simulated Service Encounters", *Interacting With Computers*, 8, 2, pp.193-206, 1996.

Banathy, B. H., *Instructional Systems*, Belmont, CA: Fearon Publications, 1968.

Betts, M., "States Bypassing Feds on Information Highways," *Computerworld*, June 20, 1994.

Bichelmeyer, B. A., Kiggins, E.A., "Using Web-based Conferencing in Post-secondary Instruction", *Proceedings of the Annual Conference on Distance Teaching and Learning*, Madison, WI, August 5-7, 1998.

Brundage, D., Keane, R., and Mackneson, R., "Application of Learning Theory to the Instruction of Adults", In Thelma Barer-Stein and James A. Draper (eds.), *The Craft of Teaching Adults*, pp. 131-144. Toronto, Ontario: Culture Concepts, 1993.

Chapin, A. L., "The State of the Internet: 1995", *Telecommunications*, Jan. 1995.

Dalton, D. W., "The Effect of Cooperative Learning Strategies on Achievement and Attitudes during Interactive Video, *Journal of Computer-Based Instruction*, 17(1), 1990.

Dick, W., and Carey, L., *The Systematic Design of Instruction* (3rd ed.), Glenview, IL: Scott, Foresman, and Company, 1990.

Duhaney, D., Technology and the Educational Process: Transforming Classroom Activities, *International Journal of Instructional Media*, 27(1), pp.67-72, 2000.

Forsyth, I., *Teaching and Learning Materials and the Internet* (2nd ed.), London: Kogan Page, 1998.

Gagne, R. M. and Briggs L. J., *Principles of Instructional Design*, Holt, Rinehart and Winston, New York, 1979.

Graham, S.W., and Wedman, J.F., "Enhancing the Appeal of Teletraining", *Journal of Instructional Psychology*, 16(4), 183-191, 1989.

Hearn G. and Mandeville T., 'The Electronic Superhighway: Increased Commodification or the Democratisation of Leisure?' *Media Information* Australia no. 75, 1995.

Ho, M. S., *Learning and Teaching in Cyberspace: An Empirical Investigation of Computer-assisted Instruction for Geography*, Academic exercise, Dept. of Geography, Faculty of Arts and Social Sciences, National University of Singapore, 1996.

Howell-Richardson, C., Mellar, H., "A Methodology for the Analysis of Patterns of Participation within Computer Communications Courses", *Instructional Science*, 24, 1, pp. 47-69, 1996.

Hudspeth, D. R., and R. G. Brey, *Instructional Telecommunications, Principles and Applications*, New York: Praeger, 1986.

Huges, K., *Entering the World-Wide Web: A Guide to Cyberspace*, Enterprise Integration Technologies, 1994.

Jones B., 'Cultural Maintenance and Change', *Media Information*, Australia. no. 69, 1993.

Jones S., 'Understanding Community in the Information Age' Cybersociety; Computer-Mediated Communication and Community, S.G. Jones (ed) Thousand Oaks CA.: Sage, 1995.

Kerr, E. Hiltz, S., *Computer-Based Instruction*, 17(1), 1982.

Kelch, P. E., Karr-Kidwell, P. J., *How Computer Technology Expands Educational Options: A Rationale, Recommendations and a Pamphlet for Administrators*, ERIC Document Reproduction Service, no. 439 668, 2000.

Lochte, R.H., *Interactive Television and Instruction*, Englewood Cliffs, NJ: Educational Technology Publications, 1993.

Martin, B. L., "Using Distance Education to Teach Instructional Design to Preservice Teachers", *Educational Technology*, Vol. XXXIV, No. 3, March 1994.

Meyrowitz. J., *No Sense of Place: The Impact of Electronic Media on Social Behaviour*, New York: Oxford University Press, 1985.

Misanchuk, E.R., "Print Tools in Distance Education", In B. Willis (ed.), *Distance Education: Strategies and Tools,* pp.109-129, Englewood Cliffs, NJ: Educational Technology Publications, 1994.

Penny. S., "Virtual Body Building", *Media Information*, Australia no. 69, 1993.

Price, R. and Repman, J., Instructional Design for College-Level Courses Using Interactive Television, *Journal of Educational Technology Systems*, 1995.

Velayo, R. S., "Supplementary Classroom Instruction via Computer Conferencing", *Educational Technology*, 1994.

Whitelock D. and Scanlon E., "Motivation, Media and Motion: Reviewing a Computer Supported Collaborative Learning Experience, In *Proceedings of the European Conference on Artificial Intelligence in Education*, P. Brna, a. Paiva and J. Self (eds)., Euro AIED, Lisbon, 1996.

Williams, M., and Paprock, K., "Instructional Design in Distance Education", *The ED Journal*, 7(4), 1994.

Wilson, A., "Instructional Multimedia in the Math Classroom and Beyond", *Paper presented at the Annual Conference of the American Mathematical Association of Two-year Colleges*, Tulsa, OK, November 3-6, 1994.

6

Millennium Education in Virtual World

Today, all aspects of human life get influenced by IT. At present majority of devices are based on digital technology. Due to technological development, the information transfer is doubling in every three years.It is important to understand that information is not education. Nor is information necessarily knowledge, although knowledge is based on information. Knowledge is an organised set of statements of facts or ideas, presenting a reasoned judgement or an experimental result and distinguish knowledge from news or entertainment though all contain information. Nevertheless, information explosion is taking place and even a literate person is feeling as if he is illiterate because he is unable to cope up with the information explosion. IT can help in coping with the information explosion.

IT is the systematic study of artifacts that can be used to give form or description to facts in order to provide meaning or support for decision making, and artifacts that can be used for the organisation, processing, communication and application of information. It is dynamic in nature. It has the potentiality to improve and manage different aspects of higher education such as teaching, professional development of teachers, sharing of resources, increasing accessibility, research and development, human resources development, total quality management, virtual university, distance education and so on.

In higher education, teaching mostly concentrates on giving information which is not the sole objective of higher education. Along with giving information, the other objectives of higher education are:

i) developing reasoning and thinking power
ii) developing judgement and decision making ability
iii) improving comprehension, speed and vocabulary
iv) developing self-concept and value clarification
v) developing proper study habits
vi) developing tolerance and ambiguity, risk taking capacity, scientific temper, etc.

Most of the teachers use lecture method which does not have potentiality of achieving majority of above stated objectives. The objectives are multidimensional in nature, so for their achievement multiple methods be used in an integrated fashion. At present IT may be of some help. IT provides:

i) access to different sources of information.
ii) information correctly, as comprehensive as possible, in different formats, with different examples.
iii) chat facility so that learners can make use of it and can exchange their ideas and views and get clarification on any topic with different experts, practitioners, etc.
iv) variety in the presentation of content which helps learners in concentration and better understanding and long retention of information which is not possible otherwise. The learners get opportunity to work on any live project with learners from other countries.
v) flexibility to learners which is denied by the traditional process and method

Many websites are available on internet freely which may be utilised by students and teachers for developing reasoning and thinking.

There was a time when society believed that teachers were born but not trained. This belief does not hold good today because there are various teacher training institutes which were established and have expanded like any other training institutes. Earlier people interested in teaching at school level were given training in different aspects of teaching but it has been expanded to all those who are teaching at the tertiary level, that is, colleges and universities.

A teacher is trained is trained for ever because there is explosion of information and knowledge due to which new disciplines are emerging. The teachers need to be trained from time to time so as to keep pace with the developments in the related areas and to work at the maximum efficiency level. It points out the need of continuous professional development of teachers.

Teachers at whatever level are considered, one finds that the number of teachers is so high that the existing training institutes at all levels cannot take care of professional development of such a large number of teachers. Some reasons for this are the following:

i) There has been no expansion both quantitative and qualitative of the existing training institutes.
ii) In certain areas even trainees are not available.
iii) The infrastructure facilities are very limited.
iv) Training is provided outside the workplace.
v) Number of training institutes is very limited. Trainees are spread all over the country.
vi) Very limited funds are available.

India can be divided into different regions and in each region a few resource centres can be established. These resource centres can be equipped with the latest technologies like, computers with internet mode, audio and video recording systems, etc. The teachers within the region can send specific requirements to the resource centre.

The resource centre can provide the required, information/ material to the teachers and colleges which help in their professional development. Further, in different subjects, the experts be identified and be asked to teach the topic(s) of their specialisation and video recording. The video cassettes can be made available to the colleges which may be used both by teachers and students.

Wherever there is a shortage of teachers, specially developed video programmes will be very useful. Wherever possible internet connections may be provided to the colleges through which teachers can be trained in its use. Some of the teachers may use this facility to update their knowledge by way of interaction with their counterparts in other foreign universities as well as Indian universities. They can get the desired information of their choice. This is required when the teacher is asked to teach a topic which he could not study while he was a student. At times the multimedia material may be available on the topic. This can be down loaded and stored in the hard-disc for future use.

Recession and investment in the field of education is decreasing globally. More funds are made available for spreading and expansion of education at lower level than at tertiary level. Thus, financial constraints have made planners, administrators, managers, and implementors to think of alternative ways and means of resource development and management.

One alternate way is to create a central facility which can be shared by students, teachers, and researchers from different departments of university where central facility has been created as well by teachers, students and researchers from other universities. This concept of resource sharing exists in India. For example, Atomic Energy and Union Grand Commission (UGC) jointly have created a central facility, called Inter University Consortium (IUC) at Indore. Internet facility is being used by doctors, teachers, researchers, etc. At present, IT seems to be the possible answer because the IT does not put any restriction on mode, type, duration, number of users, location of users, characteristics of users, and so on.

The world is becoming a small village because one can talk to any one, enter into any library, discuss on any academic problem, share any idea, seek any information, search the information which is not commonly available, etc., so that one has an access to every nook and corner of the world. All this has been made possible due to the invention of internet, e-mail, cyber cafe, etc. Recently, virtual university has come to existence. People are studying in virtual classrooms. One need not to travel to other countries and can complete education staying at own place of residence.

Anyone with internet connection can access any library whose membership is open. One can search the title of books in any subject, within a book contents can be searched, after selecting the topic, one can download it for reading, and if required one can print all the pages or even a portion of the page can also be printed. It also points out increasing accessibility to library, classroom, research organisation, etc.

Research and development (R&D) is quite common amongst industrialists, but people working in universities and research organisations are mostly conducting researches which may be fundamental research or applied research. The quality of research varies due to the disparity in available infrastructures. The universities are hardly getting any funds for carrying out research.

Majority of universities do not have linkage with industries. Therefore, industries do not fund the research activities in the university. This scenario will not continue for long due to the invention of IT. Today, it is possible to enhance research capability through the use of IT. A researcher from India can conduct research in collaboration with his/her counterparts from other countries. These days research is a team activity.

The identification of research problem, planning and carrying out can be done by pooling the wisdom of all research members of team through the use of facilities available on web. The research data sharing, analysis and interpretation has improved to a great extent. Even replication of researches has become an easy task. It has improved the reliability of research findings. Therefore, industries may start funding the researches in the universities as well as research organisations. Once research quality improves the development-based on it is bound to improve.

The material resources of any country is not unlimited but the human resource can be unlimited. The properly trained manpower can only help us in proper utilisation of the available material resources. It demands that database of trained manpower has to be developed without which the progress, growth and development of any nation is not possible and if it is so, then the speed will be slow.

At present, database of neither human resource nor material resources is available. With the development of IT, it is possible as well as feasible to have a database of human and material resources. This database can be utilised to find those areas where very little or no trained manpower is available. Not only this, even one can predict area-wise requirement of trained manpower in a stipulated time. This will help to monitor the process of development of manpower.

Today, it may not be possible and feasible for developing as well as underdeveloping nations to create infrastructural facilities for training manpower in all spheres of knowledge. If at all it is done, then the quality of infrastructure facilities may not be up to the required standard.

To develop excellent facilities, lots of funds are required, which a nation may not afford. For example, to do research of a reasonable standards, standard journals published both within the country as well as outside the country must be available for the teachers and research scholars in the university library at least. It is a well known fact that the universities are hardly in a position to subscribe three to four foreign journals in a subject due to non-availability of funds. This problem can easily be solved by the use of IT. Many journals are freely available on the internet and for others the subscription rates are very low. Similarly, IT can help any nation to get the manpower trained at a very reasonable cost.

STUDENT-CENTRED OPEN LEARNING

Institutionalised learning which is campus based, teacher based and degree based has an aura of sacresancy about it. Many students who leave school or college as dropouts or are unable to attend them due to a complexity of reasons feel hopeless, lost and isolated. To break the barriers of such isolation is the avowed objective of educational goals, reconciling opposites and paradoxes in society.

Education is a powerful medium so as to integrate and narrow down the differences between the traditional and the non-traditional, the rural and the urban the old and the young, gender differences, established methods of pedagogy and innovative or 'new' methods. The classroom has no boundaries. It can be created and typified also in newer settings and contexts. This can in very good measure reduce time, space and distance. Lifelong education is learning at any time of one's life, at any place or pace and to recreate opportunities for those who have sadly enough missed out on them. This is the dimension of educational contiguity and continuity which can attain objectives of studying need-based courses, vocational courses and professional courses.

The philosophy of education is wideranging, complex and multitudinal. Professional courses assuage the hunger of select and even elitist target groups. The so-called non-professional courses have to be contextualised in the light of the of talked about professionalism and vocationalisation of education. We have to be very careful in the usage of such terms as more often than not they tend to fragment the holistic concept of education presenting narrow frontiers to the privileged few, learning then is: to know, to do, to think and act, to learn, how to learn, to live together. Academic courses which are not popular or frowned upon, create or lead to divides and tension.

Education and its management must then reduce tension or polarities cycling at the same time what may be described as a platform of opportunities. Learning paradigms must not only create such opportunities but must also break the barriers of isolation, hurt and loneliness. They must give a beacon of hope with guts and feeling. Societies which are de-sensitised must look to education as not only a reflector of light but, as a true means to enlighten individuals with the spirit of knowledge. Knowing something, being informed about it lies at one end; applying that knowledge lies perhaps at another and constantly there are attempts towards reconciliation of such dialectical opposites and differences. Beginning with literacy at the grassroots level to higher education, the emphasis must always be on pedagogical methods which have fresh approaches, are interesting and innovative rather than simply generating information and recording such activity on paper for the satisfaction of higher authorities.

The following terms and expressions in new educational contexts are significant:

i) learner autonomy
ii) learner contiguity
iii) learner continuity
iv) lifelong learning
v) taking responsibility for one's own learning

These will help in attaining wholesome educational objectives with the help of course of zealous educational policy makers and planners. The management of education must be planned cautiously and systemically. In the overall framing of ideas enunciated above, distance education helps in narrowing the barriers of education if not actually breaking them. It also helps in capturing learning situations which are total, in conformity with the spirit of continuing and lifelong education.

Distance education and open learning keeps the very spirit of education alive thereby stultifying old attitudes, recreating them in new contexts re-establishing them with complementary and innovative devices such as tele-teaching, audio visual aids, teaching via internet facilities etc. The compartmentalisation of education has been broken and the degree bias attenuated due to the emergence of distance education and the open university as very viable, effective and composite teaching-learning systems. Teaching and learning have a mutuality and reciprocity. We have to establish such basics of educational processes if we have to view teachers and learners in new and hitherto unexamined roles. One such, is the invisibility of the teacher whether he/she is a course writer, an audiovisual script writer or a counsellor and manager. This invisibility pushes the learner to an independence and autonomy.

The strengthening of correspondence course institutes in the traditional universities will transform them into distance education directorates following the pathways of the open university methods of education. This will be an opportunistically created situation where the chances to learn will be sufficiently there for the aged, adolescents, adults, women, housewives, working men/ women etc. This is the contiguity, the time place and space continuum of education which largely hinted at earlier on.

More and more educators must learn to vigorously experiment and innovate; must also attempt to autonomise learning which is at its best when there is a high level of motivation on the part of the learner. Yet the learner always needs attention, help, guidance fostered by a spirit of empathy. The empathetic connection between the teacher and the learner is a must, it stimulates the concepts, indeed the logic of teaching-learning which at this point of time in the traditional bodies of education suffers from a very disquieting fatigue. Such fatigue needs a shot in the arm and a fillip to look at bold ways of learning.

In seeking to achieve this educational systems cannot be hermetically sealed. The prescriptive point of view must go in order to develop learner pointedness and friendly learner perspectives. What the educators want may not always be important, what on the other hand is the need of learners and target groups is paramount and as such requires critical examination. Now we come to the emphasis on training as an educational objective. To be trained, assumes a great Significance here and distance education methods of pedagogy have radicalised the concept of learning for training and upgradation purposes. Teacher education, higher education and management education can be thrust areas here.

Working people need updation in their working environments from time to time, in order to be informed of the world of work and the holistic principles that govern work and environment. Distance education, the augmentor of part-time studies, is very convenient here. Distance education and open university teaching/learning have made daunting forays into hitherto unexplored areas of teaching and learning, such as science education and technical education.

The exploration of distance education into the area of management eduction has been one of the high points of its experimentation. For examples, the IGNOU has a very popular MBA programme which has as its target groups working people with professional /managerial and supervisory experience. This is a breakaway from traditional management education which in different management institutes of the country has as its target group young graduates. The need to train and update professional skills then seriously emerges in the context of management education. Further this may also show the way for new avenues, professionally for the learner. If correspondence course directorates of universities in the country begin to offer management courses, these will no doubt be popular, through the distance education mode. However they will have to ensure the following:

i) Course quality
ii) Innovation in teaching/ learning
iii) Cost effectiveness
iv) Flexibility regarding duration, eligibility, examination etc.

Such courses may also be categorised specifically for the following target groups: young graduates without work experience and working professionals. The former hypothetically, should take care of employability and the latter of, training/professional needs. The conventional universities in the country must, come forward in this regard to give a chance to learners who are not able to make it in management institutes because of fixed criteria and severe competition. This attitudinal change in the very ethos of management education took shape in the non-formal system of education though remaining at the same time in the very sphere of higher and the university system of education.

Offering courses via the distance education system will have to take into consideration the new contextualisation of educational systems accounted for above, technology as a teaching-learning factor and the media will be the compendium of instruction and learning. The other way of looking at the problem defined here, will be to prepare modules for professionals in specialised areas. These may be short-term, capsule courses. In such a manner, we will be able to ramify the existing nature of management education and take it to learners who desire to be trained in areas of knowledge, pertaining to their work situation. Management education can be made very exciting and effective if distance education methodologies are applied to it creatively.

The science of distance education such as well written and well edited quality study material will surely be an inventive device coupled with audio-video conferencing and good audio video tapes. The philosophy of education which is now gradually taking shape into a dualistic principle, can further radicalise higher institutes of learning by introducing management education/ professional eduction/vocational eduction via distance education methods. The popularity of professional education among the employed needs to be examined in this light.

QUALITY ASSURANCE IN HIGHER EDUCATION

Quality assurance has today become a global issue with at least a few countries calling for international quality standards. Quality assessment is the evaluation of teaching and research in a specific subject. However, it is often used in an extended sense for the evaluation of an institution for overall performance, using both internal and external procedures. For effective quality assurance it is necessary to devise internal mechanisms to monitor activities, identify lacunae and shortcomings, and undertake measures that will improve performance. Every educational institution needs to establish quality assessment cells for self-evaluation and also subject itself to periodic external peer review. For effective quality assurance the aspects that need to be monitored and assessed are:

i) Infrastructure and learning resources including student support
ii) Curricula-design, content and development
iii) Teaching and learning methodologies
iv) Evaluation mechanisms and student progression
v) Linkages with research and community.

A number of performance indicators have been identified for the evaluation of the work of academic institutions and their units. These are commonly accepted as being of three types: input indicators, process indicators and output indicators. During evaluation all types need to be used in equal measure. It is necessary to carefully choose a combination of indicators that would bring out the value-added aspect of higher education.

Distance learning requires distinct indicators that bring out the effectiveness of its subsystems. An important exercise for each country, or higher education system, should be the identification of appropriate performance indicators. These need to be free from bias, relevant, verifiable, quantifiable, economically feasible and acceptable to the institution being evaluated. While identifying, or developing performance indicators institutional and national goals, need to be kept in view. Most countries have set up quality assessment agencies or institutions to monitor the performance of higher education institutions. The United Kingdom, for example, has the Quality Assurance Agency for Higher Education (QAA) for assessing the quality of teaching; and the Higher Education Funding Councils (HEFCs) for England, Wales and Scotland have been assessing the quality of research through Research Assessment Exercises. In India the assessment agencies are the National Assessment and Accreditation Council (NAAC) established by the University Grants Commission (UGC), and the National Board of Accreditation (NBA) under the All India Council for Technical Education (AICTE).

Though accreditation is at present voluntary there is a strong move to link funding with assessment. In India, NAAC is undertaking institutional evaluation which provides an assessment of the institution as a whole, but is unable to specify the quality of teaching and research in individual departments. The decision to go in for institutional evaluation has been influenced by the large number of institutions to be assessed. Departments of universities are, however, assessed by the UGC while considering cases for special assistance.

Today in the context of globalisation of education, it is necessary to ensure that the standard of education in different countries is by and large the same. **Benchmarking**, therefore, assumes significance. This is generally understood to be the process of continuously comparing and measuring an organisation, against leaders anywhere in the world, with the objective of helping the institution or organisation in taking action to improve performance. However, we may also regard it to be a way of finding and adopting best practices.

In these days, users as well as beneficiaries are not happy with the quality of higher education. It points out to the fact that there is a need to bring desirable changes in the higher education system, namely, input, process, output and feed-back. The various inputs of higher education are: the students, teachers, curriculum, infrastructure facilities, etc.

The Ministry of Human Resource Development (MHRD), Government of India, is planning to conduct one common entrance examination for selecting students for admission into various engineering colleges situated in different states of India. Selections for various posts are done by advertising the posts at national level. Thus, selections are done at the national level just to maintain the quality of input component of the system. Not only this, the curriculum is also designed by involving experts from different universities. This is again to maintain the quality of input component of the system. Teachers from different universities are invited for teaching purpose, setting and evaluating question papers, evaluating the Ph.D. thesis, conducting viva-voice, etc. All this is done with the purpose of maintaining the quality of process, output and feedback components of the system.

In spite of all this, the quality of higher education is not the same as desired by its users. One of the reasons might be the lack of continuous evaluation and monitoring of higher education system. IT can help in maintaining the total quality of me system. For example, the curriculum can be designed by updating the information through the use of internet. The opinion of experts all over the globe can be taken through the use of internet.

Each university should design the website and the complete curriculum may be made available on the website. Experts or any person visiting the website may be requested to look into the various programmes and curriculum and give suggestions as per his understanding. The person, visiting the website may also be requested to rank its programmes and curriculum. Further, the selection of teachers and students can be done with ease due to the availability of audio as well as video conferencing facilities.

Each university can select the students and teachers keeping in mind the quality of their system. The thesis can also be put on the website and people visiting the website may be asked to give observation about the thesis along with their ranks. On the basis of these, the university may decide whether the thesis be accepted or rejected.

To maintain the quality of higher education, University Grants Commission has set up the NAAC, whose purpose is Total Quality Management (TQM). At present, the NAAC Committee physically inspects the university. On the basis of their observation, the ranking of university is done. If each university is asked to develop its website and keep on updating the data in respect of different components of the system, then most probably the NAAC may not send the committee frequently to visit the university but NAAC will be able to monitor the quality of the system. NAAC may ask larger experts to give their opinion about the university after visiting the website.

The population explosion unabled universities and colleges to give admission to all those who possess minimum eligibility and desire to continue higher education. To cope up with this problem open universities and distance education departments were established. These facilities also went insufficient. Large number of foreign universities started opening their doors to people from other countries. People do take advantage of it but majority have not been able to encash it due to financial problem.

In this age of high technology people thought of establishing a university on internet which has all good features of any real university and able to eliminate all limitations of real universities, such as number of students, courses, subjects combination, holding of examination only once in annual system and with rigid schedule, unilaterality in methods of teaching; poor quality of instructional material, etc. Such a university is called virtual university.

The students can belong to any country, speak any language, may be rich or poor, etc., can be benefited from virtual university. The major requirement is the availability of the internet facility with the prospective student. Student enrolling with the virtual university can take admission in any programme provided he possesses all the essential pre-requisites of the programme. Once one is admitted he need not travel any where, and can learn any topic any where at arty time.

The prospective students do all formalities before and/or at the time of admission, namely, filling form, taking entrance examination, enrolment and/or registration, payment of fees, etc. All these have to be done online through internet from one's own place. After admission, large number of courses are available within a programme. The candidate can select any course while the number of courses is not the restriction. The only restriction is of total credits for the programme. Such a facility is not provided under the regular programmes in the traditional universities.

After selecting the courses, one can start learning any course through any method of teaching, viz., lecture method, discussion method, seminar method, self-learning, etc. The student can down load any portion of instructional material for future use. He can continue reading the same topic at any length of time and through as many methods as he wishes. It will be individualised teaching and learning rather than a group teaching as prevalent in the traditional universities. The student enrolled in virtual university can take exam at any time he likes. It will be possible to complete a programme of three years duration in two years or less. It means there cannot be age criterion to decide whether a candidate is eligible to appear in an examination.

The possibility of globalisation of education is increased with the establishment of virtual universities. Due to the inherent flexibility in Virtual University System (VUS), it will be possible to nurture the real talent of an individual. Traditional universities do not and cannot provide such a flexibility as can be done by virtual universities.

The manpower planning is poor at present because the Planning Commission hardly publishes the number of trained personnel requirement in different sectors. This will not be impossible in VUS. Thus, directly or indirectly unemployment problem of all countries can be solved by VUS. The VUS will have potentiality to offer various courses and programmes ranging from undergraduate to Ph.D., D.Sc., D.Lit., etc. It will be possible to provide courses in all branches of knowledge.

The distance education and open learning concepts were floated and different traditional universities have converted the correspondence departments into distance education departments. Both distance education departments as well as open universities are using print mode supported by video instructional material, audio material, computer-assisted instruction, internet facilities, etc., which has provided richness to the process of education and has improved the quality of education with a slight increase in cost. The audio conferencing and video conferencing are possible.

The UGC has started networking of different universities. On its completion it will be possible to share all available resources for imparting the quality of education to far distant places. Such a state has been possible only due to the development of IT and its availability all over the globe at a reasonable cost.

Nowadays, information about any area can be obtained by anyone sitting any where on the globe through the use of internet. Mostly, one has not to pay anything for down loading the information. The latest information is also available on internet. These days the foreign research journals in print form are very costly. Majority of foreign research journals are available on internet and the subscription is too low so that Indian universities can subscribe as many as they like within the available funds. Apart from internet, information is also available on compact discs (CD), audio cassettes, video cassettes, etc. All these are part and parcel of IT.

Being a materialistic society, people all over the globe want to take the maximum benefit from the available hardwares, such as, cars, telecommunications, computers, household equipments, laboratory equipments, etc. The information of latest material available in the world can be obtained by visiting various websites. The consumer can place order utilising the facility available on the internet. Now, payment can be made through internet due to the advances in e-commerce which has made the money transaction very easy and simple.

Developments in Field of Technical Education

In India, there are 662 institutions offering degree level technical education enrolling over 1.56 lakh students annually. In addition the country has 1, 171 polytechnics having a total annual intake of just over two lakh in various diploma courses. One of the main strengths of India's engineering education is that it has retained its bias for merit-based admissions, thus encouraging competitiveness. Secondly, engineering and technology education in India has constantly nurtured the science base of modern engineering, alongside core engineering courses. This has equipped our students with necessary tools for a meaningful integration of science with engineering and technology.

Modern technologies heavily lean towards scientific analysis for continued improvement in process efficiency, for a cost effective product innovation and for an overall increase in the efficacy of the system. A strong component of industrial training and project work forms an integral part of engineering curriculum, in addition to well-coordinated laboratory exercises.

Engineering education in India has received widespread recognition from the advanced nations. In fact the engineering education in the IITs and in some select institutions such as the University of Roorkee and the Delhi College of Engineering (DCE), is considered superior to many well-known universities in the advanced countries. This superiority is primarily because of the focus on quality and strict adherence to merit in admission.

The competitive edge which Indian engineering institutions have developed in engineering and technology education, has attracted foreign universities from America, England, Canada, Australia, France and Germany, to come to India, to seek students for their postgraduate and research programmes. This reflects positively on the competence of India's engineering graduates and on the capabilities of higher technical education system.

Today 662 institutions in India at degree level enrolling annually around 1.6 lakh students each year in engineering and technology courses affiliated to 248 universities around the country. A wide variation of competence and calibre is produced in the institutions. While the IITs and other reputed institutions are able to market their products in India and abroad, a large portion of engineering graduates in the country remain unemployed after leaving the institutions.

Despite having world recognition for the quality of our graduates and postgraduates, why is it that the Indian engineering institutions such as the IITs, University of Roorkee, Madras University, and Anna University, do not actively engage themselves in attracting foreign students in great numbers to these institutions? Perhaps we are allowing our territory to be visited by outside universities to take advantage of the competence which we generate in our students.

India's institutions which impart high quality under-graduate and postgraduate education, are not currently having any policy initiative to take advantage of equally bright students in other developing and developed countries, who could receive quality technical education at an affordable cost in India. Such an initiative will also reduce the burden of fees on Indian students.

The multiplicity of entrance exams which prevails in this country is another main point of concern. Even in Delhi, one has to appear in JEE for the IITs, CEE for DCE, another entrance examination for Jamia Millia Islamia in addition to combined entrance examinations for the state level colleges in various states of the country. The multiplicity of entrance examinations is in fact breaking the back of energetic school leavers who turn towards engineering education in great numbers. The students are nearly exhausted, while taking admission in an engineering institution.

The urge to pursue engineering as a career on completion of the degree programmes gradually disappears, giving rise to an intense desire to become a manager or a computer software personnel. It is high time that we resort to a single entrance examination in engineering and technology disciplines. The task appears to be monumental but is not difficult as the experience of GATE (a common entrance examination for postgraduate engineering courses conducted by the IITs) is already with us. There is at the same time an urgent need to develop updated curriculum and to reform the examination system to make it supportive of the changing global scenario to assure the quality of education as well as the relevance of the knowledge and skills.

Science base of modern engineering plays a significant role in the advancement of knowledge and its application in areas like information technology, electronics and communication, instrumentation and control, and computer engineering. In these disciplines, the scientific innovations create an urge for rapid technology change, thus providing for a greater integration of science with engineering. In areas like mechanical, electrical, chemical and civil engineering, the rapid pace to technology development necessitates a greater emphasis on interdisciplinary aspects of engineering.

The pace at which new materials are being developed based on polymers, their composites as well as the new biotechnology based intelligent material will require altogether new manufacturing technologies and would necessitate evolution of new design procedures. Such developments shall pave the way for solving the current problems of energy shortage and degradation of environment. A whole lot of exciting possibilities are awaiting the dawn of the next millennium. It is, therefore, a point to ponder as to how the quality of knowledge and skills imported to the enthusiastic school leavers in this country could be significantly improved so that, the human resource in engineering and technology produced in the Engineering institutions could meet the present and future requirements, and help build a prosperous India in the next millennium.

The University Grant Commission (UGC) plays a significant role in improving the quality of teaching and research in engineering institutions in this country as the quality of education is directly connected to the university in the country to which the courses in engineering and technology in an institution are affiliated. The quality of the course curriculum examination effectiveness are directly influenced by the efficacy and of the university academic. Unfortunately, the faculty of technology in an Indian university marked a small presence in the academic council and other bodies of the university where important decisions concerning the fate of engineering and technology education are taken.

Universities of technology such as IITs and Roorkee University have been able to sustain the growth of technology education and research and attract not only the high performer school leavers but also highly qualified and motivated faculty to join these institutions. They have been able to support the engineering and technology education at the degree level by a strong commitment to postgraduate education and research.

To support the research scientists as well as the faculty of engineering institutions and to foster research and development in areas of national relevance, the UGC has a large number of schemes such as JRF, SRF. There is a need to review the current efforts with a view to consolidate as well as to rejuvenate a greater sense of commitment in the minds of the teachers and the students in the engineering institutions towards pursuing R&D as a valid means of technology development.

At a time when multinationals and corporate houses are paying very well the bright amongst the graduates as well as assuring them with rapid career growth, the inspiration to take up teaching as career in engineering and technology is hardly visible in the well-qualified youth graduating from reputed engineering institutions in the country.

The early bird induction scheme of AICTE is a positive step in the direction of providing avenues for the talented engineering graduates to join the teaching profession. However, this scheme is still to make a real impact. What we need to do is to repeat the teachers training scheme of the 1960s which then provided a formidable support to meet the requirement of teachers in engineering institutions.

In fact, the best of the teachers in engineering institutions in India were the ones who were inducted in teaching profession through this scheme. Besides attractive rewards and merit assured career growth we have to create a high appreciation for teaching career than that prevails today what we have to do is to enthral the bright young graduates with the exciting opportunities for teaching, R&D and industrial consultancies.

The role of a teacher is vital in the growth of technical education and in upholding the quality of human resource development. What is however not unanimously upheld is the view that the teacher in an engineering institution should devote not only to teaching but also to R&D and industrial consultancy. Teaching activity should be given top priority is well understood but what is not acceptable is that the teacher teaches from the books and notes alone. The new techniques of mathematical analysis, computation, design and drafting and above all manufacturing and management technology which flood the academic world each year require teaching minds to engage themselves into an active research beyond literature surveys.

After all what is to be taught is to become relevant four years later. The teaching process has, therefore, to dynamically assimilate the growth of knowledge into its teaching methodology. If done at the level of America and Japan, the teachers in engineering institutions will be the peers of knowledge and the institutions will be the centres of not mere learning but centres of technology innovation and research. The teacher will then perform a triple role; role of a teacher, scientist and expert practising technologist simultaneously.

The ultimate beneficiary will be the students, the human capital of tomorrow. The industries will be highly benefited as they shall lean with confidence on the expertise available in the Indian institutions, and above all government shall be relieved from the fiscal contribution to R&D as the bulk of R&D in the engineering institutions will then be funded from sponsored research and industrial consultancy.

There is a feeling which persists in academic circles that diversion of efforts of a teacher towards R&D usually sacrifices teaching interest. There are teachers who are highly devoted to teaching and spend much of their spare time for preparation of teaching material and innovate in teaching to sustain interest in the class. They obviously do not have much interest in research and development which besides being time consuming deprive them of the intellectual freedom which they enjoy as teachers. R&D being time bound and result oriented demands that the teacher devoted his considerable time to the success of the work which often involves managerial functions besides expert guidance.

Being financially rewarding and a means of recognition in the profession, R&D acts as a catalyst to sustain one's interest in innovation and creative research. It also helps a faculty member aspire for a greater original contribution to the growth of knowledge and brings added satisfaction from the application of the knowledge to solve the real life problems. The teaching style of such teachers has a strong element of professional bias, highly relevant to the students who are to accept challenges in their professional career, once they leave the college. It must, however, be realised that there is a basic difference between teaching and research.

Teaching unlike research requires excellent communication skills. The interest in teaching stems from one's desire to benefit the pupils from the depth of knowledge which the teacher possesses. This interest is further enhanced if those taught respond to learning. A researcher on the other hand works himself or at the most with his team on a challenging problem and his interest in R&D is basically from the satisfaction he derives from the outcome of his research. He creates the necessary facilities for his research from sponsored research and development projects and the hard work pays in the long run as his research established him in the profession.

Students in engineering institutions are to be taught by those who take pains in sustaining the interest of the students by constantly updating their teaching material while at the same time commanding a high reputation as practising technologists, something similar to what is done in medical colleges. This requires a paradigm shift from the R&D for career prospects to R&D for national prosperity and for nurturing excellence in technical education.

The Indian government is the major financier of R&D expenditure in engineering institutions and R&D laboratories in India. The private industries only contribute less than 1.0 per cent to this vital component of economy In any case, the R&D expenditure in India is only 0.9 per cent of GNP while the developed nations spend up to 6 per cent of GNP on R&D to create a competitive edge for their innovative products. The poor spending on R&D speaks for the miserable position in respect of intellectual property generation in India. While, a higher allocation on R&D is essential, the higher technical educational institutions must perform a lot better in respect of effectiveness of their R&D activities.

With advancement in science and technology, the fast decrease in half-life of knowledge acquired and with the emerging demands for flexible human resource development, it has become absolutely essential to restructure the course curriculum, design course structure to inbuilt flexibility as also to strengthen the interdisciplinary component in engineering and technology courses. At the same time, a sound science base of modern engineering is to be provided.

Care and concern for society and environment has to become a core component of the engineering curriculum so that the engineers of today as well as the engineers of tomorrow become more responsible to the society to which they belong. They, then, in true sense, will be the pillars of strength of the economy and will be the prime movers of growth and development of a science and technology-driven economy.

The dons in the educational institutions recognise the need for assessment of skills, aptitudes and knowledge requirements of the industries and organisations which recruit their products. Currently there is a total absence of such a feedback system. The dons overwhelmingly are conscious that it is they who know the best and they alone who can decide what is best for the academics. It is this blasphemy which is responsible for the daring obsolescence of the course curriculum and a dead lock on the interaction with the industries.

The dons must understand that because of visible compulsions of global competitiveness the industries foresee the technology and human resource requirements faster than the institutions do. In fact the industries are conscious of their requirements and they gear their management to meet the challenges which the market driven economy assigns to them. The dons of the universities and colleges being self-proclaimed experts, these visionaries of growth of knowledge continue to refuse the role of the practitioners of technology in affecting the change in the academic thinking. The Indian dons are undoubtedly more sensitive in this respect than their counterparts in the advanced West where the quality and productivity have percolated in the university circles as much as in the industries.

Academic environment in an engineering institution can be effectively created if the linkages between institution and the industries are strengthened. Such linkages should provide a dynamic environment in which the expertise from the R&D could be effectively utilised by the industries and the real-life problems and prospects of the industries are taken as challenges both by the expert faculty and the students.

Presently there is a limited scope of practical experience in technical education system. This is through the laboratory exercises which are essentially aimed at illustrating the basic concepts and the vocational training by and large remains observational in nature. The effective linkages between industry and the institution could take the form of MoUs allowing each other to take advantage of and to support each other's activities.

Greater participation of students in solving the industrial problems can be ensured by designing project work in consultation with the industries. Such projects will provide a meaningful opportunity for the students to express their innotative and creative skills. The project work will thus induct the students into the research methodology even at the undergraduate level where the mind is often highly innovative and creative.

It is also highly desirable that the students are provided much greater contact hours with the experts from the industries and R&D organisations so that they can effectively interact and perceive the value of their studies. Such visits can become more meaningful if a more direct linkage is established with the selected industries and organisations. The idea should be to involve the students in the real-life situations while they are still at the studies.

Special courses with a committed intake designed specifically for the industries can also help develop the relevant human resource. The training and re-training of engineers can also be ensured through such linkages. The linkages between the institutions and the professional societies are also highly important. Such linkages shall help inculcate an attitude of professionalism in the young minds and will help the students community aspire for a contribution to the profession to which they shall rightly belong.

The problem of poor quality and remarkably high price of Indian products is perhaps an outcome of unenthusiastic technical human resource working in an uninspiring industry environment. While the technical education system has a strong bias for analysis and tutorial exorcises, it has lacked the environment for the pursuit of excellence through innovation and creativity. It has not fully exploited the mental capabilities of its students nor has it given them the orientation necessary to enhance one's commitment to the cause of technology development for the betterment of the quality of life of the people of their country.

The management of higher technical education in India has by and large lacked the appreciation of the role of the teachers, its faculty in the over all development of the institutions. It has lacked in emphasis on people's development and it has cared least for nurturing an environment for the development of an individual.

The quality improvement programme of the 1970s and 1980s has, no doubt, improved the qualifications of the faculty but it has not largely benefited the institutions academic or research programmes primarily because of lack of peer pressure on such individuals. They also lacked motivation to improve the institutions, laboratories and work environment.

The management and the teachers still remain at loggerheads in respect of their expectations and aspirations. There is no meeting of the minds between the objectives of the institution and the growth and advancement of the faculty members.

The educational institutions in the higher technical education sector have to ensure that they have in their faculty and staff people who are world class having calibre and competence to remain knowledge workers throughout their working life. To cater for this requirement, the style of management has to undergo a clear re-orientation in respect of:

i) recognition of achievements
ii) empowerment of an individual
iii) identification of talent
iv) respect for one's capabilities
v) motivation for continuous upgradation of skills.

Management of technology change has already become a formidable challenge to the industries as well as the engineering institutions. This has brought to the forefront an urgent need to focus our attention on the management of knowledge and expertise. The management of innovation requires a national initiative, formulation of globally compatible policies and evolution of practices and procedures to harness Indian genius in engineering and technology sectors. Technical education and research has a prominent role to play in the growth of the economy and in the rapid technoeconomic development of the country.

EDUCATION MANAGEMENT

The new millennium promises to herald a different environment for human development in all walks of life, including education. Among numerous new ingredients of the environment, a very potent one will be knowledge. It is going to be a knowledge-driven century with all its implications. Education being a service, based on knowledge, past, present and future, its entire field is going to be tremendously influenced by the knowledge-saturated environment of the new millennium.

Education, and all related activities like teaching, learning, evaluating research, materials production, management of education etc., will, therefore, have to prepare themselves to meet the knowledge-driven socio-cultural environment that will emerge year after year in the 21st century. Who will bear this heavy cross? In reality, all stake-holders in the enterprise of education—policy makers, curriculum framers, teachers, principals, deans, education managers, evaluators, research workers and students—will be required to bear this cross.

Principals and deans, as managers, will be required to lead their institutions into that challenging environment—the knowledge-driven environment, with all its implications. The principals and deans are leaders and managers of education in action, in their institutions and in society at large.

The educational institution of the new millennium is being visualised as a place where knowledge will be generated, where knowledge will also be refined and reinvented, where knowledge will be examined, explored and restated, where knowledge will be acquired by both teachers and students, where knowledge will be shared by the community, and where knowledge will be transformed into experience, into action, into wisdom, into vision and in one form or another. It will be institution without walls, pulsating with new dynamics of freedom, self-inquiry, self-exploration, self-management, self-evaluation, an un-restricted pursuit of knowledge, with or without any outside aid. The teacher will no longer be a source let alone the only source, of all knowledge and wisdom, but will only be a fellow- traveller, a co-worker, at times a role-model, at times a guide, a facilitator on the path to self-unfolding.

The education manager of the new millennium could provide effective leadership, he should be a perceptive, imaginative, enterprising, proactive and sensitive education manager. He must have a clear vision of the institution of education and his assignment of the new millennium. Only a system with vision, people with vision, and programmes with vision, shall survive in the new millennium. The vision shall comprise the following components:

i) *A human system*: He shall view the institution as a comprehensive human organisation in all its implications.

ii) *A thinking system*: He shall head an organisation with its own mind, a thinking body in all respects, which evolves its own thoughts, and imaginations continually.

iii) *A responding system*: He shall head a sensitive human body, which gets sensitised, conscientised and humanised and which feels and responds to others empathetically.

iv) *A learning system*: He shall deal with an organic system whose senses work, absorb, adjust, redefine, change and assume new forms. It continually sheds obsolescence and acquires newness and freshness.

v) *A pro-active system*: His shall be an institution that shall take action and initiative to push ahead on its own in an all-emerging scenario.

vi) *A global system*: His institution will have both local and global orientations in visualising its roles, tasks and functions and transacting them with commitment.

viii)) *A productive/creative system*: His organisation comprising people, programmes, activities, materials, dreams etc, shall be maximally productive in all respects; productive of knowledge, ideas, services, etc.

The education manager of the new millennium should have a good mission, a commitment, a covenant to identify with, to work for, to strive for, and not to relent till it is achieved fully. The institute of the new millennium is supposed to have seven missions. They are:

i) *To do human resource development*: It is the entire gamut of human development that will be the mission of the institution to realise.

ii) *To make learning self-fulfilling*: Learning shall be freed from rote, imitation, repetition, regurgitation, manipulation and other dependence. It shall be an enterprising adventure, open, multi-sourced, creative and life-fulfilling.

iii) *To establish synergy between education and technology*: Education shall be technology-savvy, and, therefore, enormously strengthened with alternatives open for learners to learn, to generate knowledge.

iv) *To turn education into a socially sensitive pursuit*: The institution and its programmes will be wedded to society; to seek answers to social concerns; and to empower society through knowledge, its products and service.

v) *To promote merit, quality and excellence*: To meet the challenges of life governed by modern science and technology and challenged by myriad problems of human development, education shall have to equip learners with quality achievement in all respects.

vi) *To make R&D an integral part of the system*: Education in the new millennium should be a self-renewing force. That will require R&D support in various forms in its diverse pursuits.

vii) *To make the future happen*: The education manager shall have to be a futurologist in action. He must both anticipate the future scenario and make the perceived future take shape through his imagination, inspiration, leadership and managerial competence.

A sound strategy comprises convergence of methods, means, and materials, and coordination, and pooling of components is necessary to the accomplishment of a vision and carrying out of a mission with fervour and dedication. The seven components of the strategy in question consist of the following:

i) *To professionalise the entire enterprise*: The education manager will have to infuse professional attitudes, approaches, behaviours and relationships in all aspects of education—teaching, learning, testing, human relations etc. He will need to take care to give a human face to all the dealings.

ii) To benchmark all endeavours: He will have to establish high templates, develop competitive edge, press R&D activities and make the entire environment quality-bound. He will have to set up a brand name and never to compromise on these issues in anyway.

iii) *To autonomise the system*: He will have to liberate, deregulate, dehierarchise, delegate, and recognise the smallest share, accept alternative routes, provide freedom to think, to differ, to decide, to withdraw, to innovate and to experiment.

iv) *To transparentise top down*: He will have to build a climate of openness, frankness, involvement and participation; and let all have the right to know and to give opinion on. This will equalise all.

v) *To multi-source the system*: A knowledge-based society should have alternative sources for knowledge inputs—people, media, IT, ideas, suggestions. Any individual, whatever his station, is not the sole source of wisdom or strength. The education manager shall pool the community reservoir, technology reservoir and even the traditional folk-knowledge reservoir.

vi) *To network all humans and the system*: The manager should realise that the world is getting wired. So he must network people, ideas, resources, and practices. He should form human teams as well as non-human clusters. He should form webs.

vii) *To operate on a fast track*: The new millennium will be an age of fierce competition, therefore one must be just in time for everything—a reform, an experiment, a product, a programme, an innovation or a change. The education manager must do time management. He must also do crisis management as well as trouble management.

The new millennium needs students as knowledge workers, rather than subservient, uncommitted, non-productive, uncreative robots that carry out tailor-made tasks based on rote-ability. It needs generators of knowledge, creators of knowledge, adventurers of knowledge and self-learners with skills to operate in a competitive world. So we should revisualise education management leadership. It's a broad-based human resource development related leadership. The action plan shall have to be developed cooperatively by involving society, education trusts and corporate bodies, parents, teachers and, of course, students.

REFERENCES

Ackermann, E., *Tools for Teaching: The World Wide Web and a Web Browser*, 1996.

Aronowitz, S., *The Knowledge Factory: Dismantling the Corporate University and Creating True Higher Learning*, Boston: Beacon, 2000.

Betts, M., "States Bypassing Feds on Information Highways", *Computerworld*, June 20, 1994.

Dede, C. J., "The Future of Multimedia: Bridging to Virtual Worlds, *Educational Technology*, 1992.

Khanna, S.K., "Challenges of Higher Technical Education in India", *Convocation Address*, DCE, Sept. 1993.

Kochmer, J., *Internet Passport: Northwestnet's Guide to Our World Online*, Bellevue, WA: NorthWestNet and Northwest Academic Computing Consortium, Inc. (http://info.nwnet.net/passport), 1995.

Kraft. P and Truex D., "Postmodern Management and Information Technology in the Modern Industrial Corporation" R. Baskerville, S. Smithson, O. Ngwenyama and J.I DeGross (eds.) *Transforming Organisations with Infor nation Technology IFIP*, 1994.

Portway, P., and Lane, C., *Technical Guide to Teleconferencing and Distance Learning*. San Ramon, CA: Applied Business telecommunications, 1992.

Turlington, S., *Walking the World Wide Web*, Ventana Press, 1995.

Winn, W. and Bricken, W., "Designing Virtual Worlds for Use in Mathematics Education: The example of Experiential Algebra, *Educational Technology*, 1992.

7

Teacher Education and Virtual Games

Long before a child enters a formal class/school/ he has already been guided, coached and instructed in varying degrees. Therefore, a teacher is not new to her/him but now his/her functions are very well-defined be it learning or teaching. If the earlier form of teaching/instruction was not tantamount to being called 'tuition' the latter in the classroom situation is definitely 'tuition' in every sense of the term.

In a formal classroom the teacher is told what to teach and which skills to offer and for the services rendered what to expect in return, no such conditions are operant during the pre-schooling days. Now all this is too wellknown to be repeated/elaborated. It implies that we are aware that teaching per se is both voluntary and involuntary.

When we go voluntarily for learning we are quite sure what we want and how much we want and at the same time there are choices. These choices are not restricted to the areas of interest, levels of learning or even the modes of acquisition. An individual volunteers to learn classical music, painting or some form of performing art. Implicit in this position is the choice of area, quality and level of learning, the duration and necessary discipline needed besides the effort and money one will have to invest.

In involuntary learning, one has no choices, gradations or even matching interests. This kind of learning is determined by the situation one is placed in. For instance, a child learns from his siblings not because he has volunteered, or, from one's parents not because of his choice, or, has to go to a certain type of school because the society cannot offer a better alternative etc. The nature of involuntariness could also be predetermined by one's normal or abnormal birth.

The political formation of a country may also play a decisive role in these choices. For instance, a democracy offers choices which a dictatorship does not. A religious, non-secular society will inevitably result in fundamentalist teaching and moral code. A Taliban cannot help being Taliban because of his early involuntary compulsions. Later on beyond his *madrasah* walls his conditioning makes it impossible for him to deny any of his teachings what was once his forced choice now becomes his mission in later life. His learning is, therefore, conditioning in which his maturation, choices etc., have played an insignificant role as compared with the external circumstances which eventually carried the day.

When we choose a democratic form of society we face numerous questions and in most cases the answers one has to give oneself. Freedom of choice, as acknowledged universally, is serious business. All societies evolve alternatives and find norms of achievement. A nation's history could in a limited manner determine its present.

For instance, India's ancient past is as much alive today as its medieval character. While India is modernising, changing and even globalising we should not forget that India's educational system continues to reflect its past. Indeed, Indian education along with its arts and culture have continued to reflect its ancient traditions.

Today, India faces the problems teacher education which are unbelievably insurmountable. We may however, not overlook the reality. The fact is that teacher training has legal sanction and also a legal status. This cannot be changed. But this is also true that no nation has so far evolved an ideal form of teacher training. While most of the problems in this area are nation-specific, a few are of universal dimensions.

If it is information area it is equally suitable to face-to-face mode as well as correspondence distance education mode. If not, distance education is not suited for this training. And if one has to have a proper mix of both one should think or training surgeons through some distance education mode and then decide the proportion of time allocated for its mode or practice. This is illogical, a teacher's job in a teachers' college, therefore, deserves to be looked at rather closely.

The social origins of teachers are mostly lower or lower middle class. Unfortunately, in the developed world the social origins of teacher's have been adversely commented upon. To talk of Indian teachers in this light at any period of time may not be liked by all. Perhaps, it is not very surprising that teachers do not appear to be either very independent, innovative or even enterprising. Indeed, teaching as a profession in India is basically conservative, conformist and extremely submissive.

The association of university departments with teacher training has distorted the entire perception. What started as a short-term skill training course once, has now become a full-blown information-based and highly theoretical area. The tragedy is that the theoreticians are neither competent theorisers nor knowledgeable, or even well informed beings.

The British in India had a political agenda in education to guide them. This is not borne out either by the writing of Jawaharlal Nehru who called British rule 'fortuitous' or even K.M. Panikkar's *Asia and Western Dominance* which is equally categorical about their lack of any design. For these scholars Macaulay's *Minutes* decided the medium of instruction in schools and not the universal law that the ruled always learn the language of the rulers. The American hegemony has proved that today American literature is as necessary to read as the English was once.

In India the Muslims had no set agenda of governance or of education but statistics show that in *madrasahs* Hindus outnumbered Muslims and the Brahmins and Kayasthas learnt Persian and Arabic both. Arabic is the language of theologians. No one has tried to find out the basic cause or discover a Macaulay behind all this and there is no proof that either the Mughals /Turks /Slaves had any political agenda to guide their educational effort.

In fact the Indian rate of literacy during British rule was much higher than that of their rulers back home; our social norms were not as poor as theirs and that colonisation has its own logic which both the colonisers and the colonised follow. With no knowledge of British history any interpretation of British rule in India would be least dependable.

Indians are consciously trying to indigenise teacher education. However mental acrobatics of a few do not disprove the fact that Indian scholar ship in teacher education is borrowed, stale, infantile and even ludicrously elementary. Rejected ideas of the West are implemented in their dying state in India and acclaimed as feats of achievement. The pity is that Indian teacher educators at the university level show neither imagination, nor any concern for improving their area.

Indian teacher educators have no heights to ascend and none to compete with or model skills to copy. Indeed, they have set no standards of their own to compare with. Therefore, they take up issues and deliver judgments without any shred of evidence. In no other academic area can one hold out theory or deliver a judgment without credible research.

Indeed, the type of research teacher education in India thrives on has few country-specific issues or problems. Since they teach borrowed ideas, they borrow areas for research too. A few exceptions are noteworthy but even for those areas such as adult education, non-formal, tribal education or rates of literacy the inspiration is foreign in origin. Even such areas like Indian philosophy, logic, etc., which have a hoary history to back up, we have produced no work to match either J.S. Brubacher or R.S. Peters. We do not use any Indian psychology or its ancient classifications in education.

India has a classical tradition of training teachers. Unfortunately, that training has nowadays got restricted to the training of priests—Hindu, Muslim and Christian. One needs to study this training purely from a secular, functional and curiosity point of view. We are not quite sure how instructive it may eventually prove to be. We need to do a lot in this regard and overcome the hesitation of entering an unexplored area.

India has a numerous institutions engaged in training their personnel ranging from business, industry, management to smaller trades and practices. Teachers are trained for educating all varieties of handicapped children—visual, physical, mental, etc., besides for all the possible levels of education starting with nursery to higher and for all kinds of specialisations like physical education, nursing, medicine, engineering, etc. If one looks at the scenario one has a feeling that while the canvas is large, the collage is confusing and very restricted in vision and practices.

The teachers' training programmes in India lacks understanding and insight into the attributes/qualities which we would wish our future teachers to possess. It fails to relate each prescribed lesson with the expectations we have from them. In a way this programme is carried on because we have not outgrown our mental sloth of carrying on with the drudgery allocated to us as part of our history.

We must remember there is future as, well, if there is past. No one can go on living in a cuckoo's land forever. We should be able to analyse the textbooks and reference material very closely because if we ever did we would be surprised that if there is any area wherein non-changers are heartily welcomed it is India's teacher education programme.

Teacher education in India borrows ideas, translate materials and adjust Indian material to Western ideologues. If all this is not good, the same could be said about several current practices. What is being pleaded here is the rationale behind product evaluation of teachers' colleges, rating scales for concepts, and practices besides determining the duration for training etc., to guide our future efforts.

Teachers in India perform jobs which teachers elsewhere are not expected to undertake. The job requirement must take precedence over theorising, and country-specificity should take priority over unnecessary globalisation. Education unlike business or industry competes with others only in a very restricted sense. Most of our teachers will never cross borders and would not need theories which have no bearing on their day to day requirements.

Nowadays, changes have been sought to be introduced in the preparation of teachers. The stress has been on the change of curriculum, lengthening of the duration of training and suggestion for overall quality improvement through enforcing building, equipment, library, and teacher-pupil ratio norms. Perhaps norms are necessary in every walk of life but when norms take on the shape of immutable laws with the big brother watching you against defaults, education and the military careers start appearing identical.

In this Info-age we have conquered time and distance, the sea and sky. Information is a diverse, dynamic and inexhaustible source that affects all disciplines and lives of people. The UNESCO world conference on Higher Education proclaimed that education is a fundamental pillar of human rights, democracy, sustainable development and peace. The draft proposal on higher education for 21st century envisages the quality of higher education as a multidimensional concept and institutions in higher learning must play a role in identifying and addressing the issues that affect the well being of communities and global society.

Higher education institutions should no more be considered as the traditional teaching centres but they must be recognised as learning organisations. Teacher education consists of all formal and informal activities; and experiences that help to qualify a person towards assuming and discharging the responsibilities more effectively, efficiently and successfully. The educational system in India today is at a critical state with more resistance to absorb the significant changes taking place in the modem society. The societal needs are acquiring more and more knowledge in less and less time. The transformation that society is going through demands rejuvenation in the way we teach and it is more important than what is taught.

In order to prepare ourselves, for the dawn of the twenty first century, the educationists have to give a plan to shoulder the responsibility of moulding the character of society according to the societal needs of the day. Good teacher education curriculum aims at the development of balanced personalities who are culturally refined, emotionally stable, ethically sound, intellectually alert, socially efficient, spiritually upright and physically strong.

The three basic responsibilities of teacher eduction are: teaching, research and extension; and they must be reflected in every phase of our educational system. As information technology has caused many changes in the communication network system, teaching at all levels must be modem, innovative and concurrent with the latest developments to face the emerging challenges of the future. To cope up with the challenges of changes in the fast changing world order, teachers must have desired theoretical knowledge, skill orientation, linguistic ability, pedagogical skills, management skills, and accountability. Professional education of teachers and Professionalism in teachers determine the teaching behaviour and teachers' behaviour respectively.

Curriculum in teacher education refers to all the courses, collectively offered in a subject. The teachers have to be trained while their preparation depends upon the teacher education curriculum. The university implies the universality of knowledge or universalism of relevance and therefore the curriculum should reflect the social needs. The effectiveness of the professional preparation of teachers rest on broad-based curriculum for teacher educators. A stagnant and static system of eduction cannot tolerate a dynamic teacher, an irrelevant system of education cannot permit a teacher to make teaching relevant to the needs of the present learners or the modem society. Besides, the subject oriented system of examination cannot create good opportunities to the teachers who want to promote a sound philosophy of life to build integral personality of the learners.

There is a hue and cry from the educational planners that the existing curriculum in teacher eduction is out moded, unwieldy, inflexible and does not meet the demands of the contemporary society. The syllabi place maximum premium on bookish knowledge rather than help the teacher educators to develop the different skills of teaching.

A good teacher education curriculum must have the following bearings:

i) It has to enlarge the prospective teachers' know edge base.
ii) It has to develop and improve the teaching skills of the teacher educators and
iii) It is a system that has to respond to the challenges of the modem society.

At present, the teacher education curriculum the traditional concept of instruction both in terms of its contextual organisation and instructional procedures used in the class room conditions. It does not possess any adjustment mechanism for the changed concept of instruction resulting from new curriculum.

The present teacher education curriculum fails to develop a sense of commitment and aspects of moral and legal accountability. Moral accountability is based upon a sense of responsibility—a feeling that one is responsible to students, parents colleagues and oneself. Legal accountability on the other hand refers to one's employer in terms of fulfilling the terms and conditions of service. The main purpose of teacher education is to prepare the teachers with educated minds coupled with training in teaching skills.

Today, the teacher education curriculum is burdened with too much of theoretical treatment. The large component of theory papers accommodated in the teacher education curriculum has retarded the growth of practical and pedagogical aspects of the programme. This in turn has checked the growth of teacher education as an exclusively professional course.

The major challenge to teachers and other educators today is the challenge to change and innovate. There are four dimensions of curriculum:

i) Structure related dimension
ii) Content related dimension
iii) Transaction related dimension and
iv) Curriculum related process dimension

Structure related dimension heavily weighs in favour of theory, resulting in low effectiveness of teacher education programme. The curriculum framework developed by the NCTE lays emphasis on pedagogical theory working with community and content-cum-methodology in order to provide maximum weightage to the practical side of the teacher education.

The core of the content related dimension covers the facts, concepts, generalisation, skills, values and attitudes. A notable shift in the treatment of the contents to suit to the emerging trends in the society is observed in this phase of dimension of curriculum.

The transaction related dimension of teacher education deals with the aspects of implementation. The teaching strategies employing media and material used for effective curriculum transaction form the core of this dimension.

The fourth dimension is curriculum development process which refers to curriculum drafting, evaluation restructuring and decision making process. These trends need to be strengthened as they will improve the quality of curriculum transaction, in addition to the improvement in the preparation of quality of instructional materials.

It is likely to improve and strengthen the teacher education programme in a global perspective. The best available brains in the country should be inducted in teaching profession to entrust with the responsibility of creating, codifying and disseminating knowledge for the training of man power for the future. Television can bring the world into a class room and the cyber class room to the door steps of a learner. This audio-visual media is capable of creating an impact on its learners because of their accessibility, availability and acceptability. The best teacher educators can be selected to take part in audio-visual programmes as resource persons and their expertise could be made available to many students at a time. The audio-visual programmes can be planned and produced in different formats like discussion, dialogue, interview, feature and documentary incorporating all the socially relevant aspects of Indian life. Teleconferencing is another tool at the disposal of the distance educators to impart learning towards orienting the learners to the effective multicultural education.

The World Wide Web has obliterated the geographical boundaries. Information and stored knowledge across the world are now at mouse-click distance and access is almost instantaneous. A creative and committed teacher is always more in demand than anything else though computers are used in the class room situation to help the teacher to fulfil the goal of making, all the students understand the concepts very clearly and more effectively. Classical teachers should not have any apprehension that computer will replace the teachers making them redundant. Computer Assisted Learning (CAL) will relieve drudgery of the teachers and the teacher educators must have a positive attitude towards the utilisation of computer to reach the unreached learners in the journey of learning. Languages are not only the subjects of knowledge but a means of knowledge. English should be taught as a language of global communication and that can also be used to impart certain skills and values such as scientific vision and universal brotherhood.

Restructuring of curriculum and updating syllabi of teacher education must take into account the following:

i) high degree of professionalism
ii) vanishing disciplinary boundaries and
iii) social relevance.

NET-SURFING

According to the NASSCOM Survey (Mehta, 2000), there are more than 3.7 million Indians use internet. Though only 11.3 per cent, educational use of Internet is second largest, second to general information seeking. The use of Internet is fast expanding; more than 81 per cent personal computers sold during the financial year 1999-2000 were driven by needs to access internet.

Effective teaching is possible only when teachers themselves up-to-date on a subject. Conventionally, teachers resort to printed literature in the form of books and articles. In case of research, reviewing the important relevant literature related to the problem under study is almost magnum opus. The review involves abstraction of earlier research studies, theoretical articles, and papers of important authorities in the field from books, journals, abstract-journals, encyclopaedia, etc. This manual search is laborious and time consuming. Online search on Internet has made retrieval of information and referencing far easier for the teachers as well as researchers. Teachers of higher education, can access wealth of information on any subject—latest research, developments and publications in minutes if not seconds from all over the world. Online searches are very cost effective; a teacher and researcher need not travel to libraries within the city or outside the city to collect information.

Internet surfing implies venturing out to explore with or without any particular destination in mind. We just browse through the contents and move to some other destination. World Wide Web (WWW) is the easiest and most popularly used browsing mechanism on the Internet. Web is the most popular format for storing and retrieving information; it provides instant and unlimited access to online resources.

Today, there are millions of sites on the WWW. We need not take permission from anyone to store or retrieve information. There are several types of sites. Universities and institutions maintain Home-pages. Many individuals and groups maintain their personal or group sites. Full text papers/research articles are available on these sites. These can be downloaded free of cost from these sites and used as references.

Search engines are the gateways to information on the Internet. They are capable of accessing information from the WWW based cataloguing systems. Some of the popular Search Engines are yahoo, google, etc. These are called search engines because they search large databases on WWW addresses based on key words they find in documents stored on the Web. Its use is very simple. Once we open the Internet, we type, e.g. www.google.com. Within seconds, the computer terminal displays the google page, and displays a small window with two panes. One pane asks for key words. And, second pane asks for the language, if the Search Engine is multilingual.

In India, Internet was supported earlier by the government—Videsh Sanchar Nigam Limited (VSNL) was the sole vendor. But now it has been privatised. Quiet a few government and private companies offer Internet facilities at competitive rates, e.g. MTNL, Satyam, Mantra Online, and many more. Though as a marketing strategy companies like Dishnet are providing free Internet facility to women and children, the rates are extremely competitive. Also, the Internet prices are packaged differently by different companies. Major criteria are fixed period unlimited time, fixed number of hour without fixed period and fixed number of hour in fixed period. Nevertheless, on an average it costs about Rs. 3000.00 for 500 hours in a year. There are smaller chunks like 100 hours or 50 hours for lower prices. Average cost of use of Internet per hour, hence, is approximately, Rs. 6.0.

For Internet access, we need only a computer with Internet connections and a telephone facility. Local Telephone is enough to access information anywhere in the world. First connection is established with the server at the VSNL or MTNL or Satyam Online or Mantra Online which are within the city. It is that server which connects to the world. All universities and almost all colleges have computers and telephone facilities. With minor investment of about Rs. 1000.00 per year for the Internet connection, our teachers in higher education can have access to this important academic and professional resource.

There are several teething and recurring problems on internet. One of the major problems is getting connected to the Internet server. In peak office hours it is extremely difficult to get connected. More important problem is remaining connected or online. While we are at the midst of our search, the line may get disconnected. Modems pose another set of problems. The internal modem at times are not dependable; external modems are clumsy and difficult to manage. Internet has tremendous power to detract. One may land up on a site with almost all major US newspapers. The cricket fans can get hooked to Internet. But more serious problem is the volume of data generated by such searches. Very often the search informs thousands and lakhs of entries. The most difficult problem is to browse and choose the relevant ones from a such a large volume of data. The only way to reduce is to narrow down the scope by stringently selecting the key words and defining the years of the records.

VIRTUAL GAMES

Educational and training organisations have invested significantly in the development, support, and management of online learning environments. Yet as they move into the implementation phase, there are mixed reports about the effectiveness of these environments. While instructional designers are showcasing outstanding successes, many online training products are gathering dust on virtual shelve. Attracting learners, trainers, and other stakeholders to adopt an online learning environment seems a like handing out samples of a new product line in a supermarket. While enough learners enrol in online courses a successfully complete them, others do not stay return. Keeping learners from dropping out is a challenge for many online facilitators and trainers.

Instructional designers are currently exploring strategies for motivating learners to not only come but also stay, contribute, and return to the world of online learning. This article focuses on one particular, perspective: how to encourage person-to-person interactivity with a games-based methodology that uses e-mail.

Most people promote interactivity as the most valuable feature of online learning. However, closer look at many instructional offerings online, reveals that much of this interactivity merely connects the learner with the content. We do not believe this is enough. Neither does rigorous research. Most online environments overlook communication technologies like e-mail, forums, and chat as potential learning technologies. These technologies offer unique opportunities for supporting learner-to-learner and learner-to-facilitator interaction that encourage higher-order cognitive skills, such as application, analysis, and synthesis.

Through the use of open-ended and often provocative questions, virtual games are a challenging way to create and process content, check and assess participant understanding, use role play and simulations to solve problems, make decisions, and provide feedback.

E-mail game, a facilitator and a group of players address a key issue by sending and receiving messages during several rounds of play spread over days or weeks. Typical e-mail games may exploit the ability of the internet to ignore geographic distances and capitalise on the ability of participants to generate and process content. In the early rounds of play the interaction is between players and the facilitator, while in later rounds, players come together to discuss processed content and to debrief the process. E-mail games are being used for benchmarking and idea-sharing activities.

Today most of the virtual games have been played in a professional development context. The LearnScope Virtual Learning Community (www.learnscope.anta.gov.au). (LearnScope is an Australian national professional development programme) aimed to encourage teachers and trainers in the vocational education and training sector to utilise online technologies to achieve more flexible learning. There are three type of e-mail games are with them.

i) *Depolarise:* This role-playing game uses e-mail and a bulletin board. Depolariser is based on the philosophy that many issues that we treat as problems to be solved are actually polarities to be managed. During the six rounds of the game, players explore this issue from both a personal perspective and also from a designated role. By informing the players about the range of positions, we increase their awareness of the spread of opinions around the issue. The game typically encourages players at extremes to get closer to the average.

ii) *Galactic wormhole.* This is a role-play game, players participate in a time-travel scenario to explore an issue relevant to their context. Each player is given either a utopian scenario in the form of a newspaper headline or a dystopian scenario. Players are randomly assigned one of these two scenarios and given one of five stakeholder roles of trainer, learner, manager, decision-maker, or industry client. Each player is then asked to submit a 150-word story outlining how his or her stakeholders contributed to either this utopian or dystopian future. These scenarios are submitted anonymously to the facilitator who collates and posts them in a forum. After reviewing all the optimistic and pessimistic scenarios, players submit their five top ideas for ensuring a utopian future. Finally, players vote on critical issues that need to be addressed to ensure the utopian future.

iii) *C3PO.* This acronym C3PO stands for *Challenge, Pool, Poll, Predict,* and *Outcome*. In Round 1 of C3PO, players receive an open-ended challenge Each player sends three ideas to meet this challenge. In Round 2, the facilitator sends the resulting pool of ideas to the players and asks them to generate a priority list. Players read through the pool of ideas, select the three that personally appeal to them most, and send them to the facilitator. In Round 3, players review the original pool of ideas and make a prediction of how the entire group would have voted, and identify the top set that would have received the most votes. During the selection process in Round 2, the players consider how they personally feel and react to the ideas. During the prediction process in Round 3, the players put themselves in other players' positions and estimate the reaction of the population. As one player put it, "The prediction step forces you to stop thinking wishfully, projecting your preferences, and become absolutely objective." The player with the closest prediction is the winner.

From player comments during and after each e-mail game, we have identified these emerging factors to be explored in greater depth:

i) *E-mail is familiar, available, cost-effective, and widely used:* User confidence with e-mail means the focus can be on the learning process without players being distracted by unfamiliar technology. E-mail is very inclusive, as online novices and experts can participate on an equal footing.

ii) *E-mail comes to the desktop*: No passwords are needed and there are no download hold-ups. The game is integrated with the daily work of players, minimising the effort required for participation.

iii) *E-mail games promote more effective learning:* This person-to-person approach is different from the person-to-computer methods used for many electronic games. The games require active participation as players must generate and process the content.

iv) *E-mail games transcend space and time constraints:* The distributed asynchronous process permits colleagues anywhere in the world to share their expertise and to address common issues. Several of our games have involved players from the US, Australia, Greece, Canada, France, India, Poland, Israel, Argentina, Mexico, and the United Kingdom. As the deadline for each round contains sufficient number of days, players at different time zones can arrange their participation to suit their personal schedules.

v) *Players can be anonymous:* This aspect of e-mail games attracts participation by many people who normally lurk. Anonymity allows people to be more candid and extreme in their opinions without fear of reprisal or ridicule. We have also effectively used play names to increase this anonymity.

vi) *E-games achieve productive outcomes*: These games generate ideas, solve problems, and encourage dialogues on topics and issues that are relevant and salient to the participants.

vii) *E-mail games are continuously improved:* The built-in iterative feedback process through structured debriefing provides dynamic formative evaluation for immediate refinements that even better meet user needs.

E-mail games are easy to adopt and adapt. The templates for these games are deliberately designed to permit easy replacement of old content with new: The content changes, but the process stays the same. Once players have participated in a game, they can easily modify it for use in their own context. However, there is much more to a successful e-mail game than plugging in new content and knowing that the process will work.

A successful virtual game is effective facilitation. Although players generate and process the content, the facilitator orchestrates the game. To provide a seamless virtual game, facilitation requires, technical, administrative, interpersonal, and instructional design functions.

Facilitators need a working knowledge of the communication technologies they will be using to play virtual games as well as spreadsheets for data management. If players experience technical difficulties or get confused with the forum software, they will most often turn to the facilitator for assistance. Developing a FAQs file allows the facilitator to be responsive to most queries.

As responses to e-mail games arrive, they must be processed quickly and accurately in preparation for the next round of play. Accurate and systematic recordkeeping, like player tracking, collation of input, and sending out of next rounds are critical to the smooth flow of e-mail games.

While the game templates provide the steps needed to play a game, facilitating a game is more than a mechanical process. Setting the scene, sustaining motivation, and debriefing relies on the human factor and a fair degree of interpersonal skill. Facilitators need to monitor the progress of a game and determine when to change the pace, contact individual players, and change the tone of the play. Some players reply promptly, others leave it to the last minute, some miss rounds, and some register but never contribute.

Virtual games require a dynamic instructional process. The facilitator is close to the players and in a position to be responsive to feedback. As the games are played in rounds, it is easy to use a just-in-time instructional design process.

REFERENCES

Albrecht, R., Bardsley, G., *Strategic Planning and Academic Planning for Distance Education*, in B. D. Willis (ed.), *Distance Education: Strategies and Tools,* pp. 67-85, Englewood Cliffs: Educational Technology Publications, 1994.

Alcord, B., and Wittgen, A., "The Authority to Think: The Student-centred Classroom", *Contemporary Education*, 61(2), 1990.

Aronowitz, S., *The Knowledge Factory: Dismantling the Corporate University and Creating True Higher Learning*, Boston: Beacon, 2000.

Auter, P. I., Hanna, M. S., "The Challenge of Developing Online Courses", *Paper presented at the Annual Meeting of the Speech Communication Association*, San Diego, CA, November 23-26, 1996.

Barrett M. Sahay S. Walsham G., "Understanding IT and Social Transformation: Development and Illustration of a Conceptual Scheme", *Proceedings from the 17th International Conference on Information Systems (ICIS'96)*, 1996.

Beare, P.L., "The Comparative Effectiveness of Videotape, Audiotape, and Telelecture in Delivering Continuing Teacher Education, *American Journal of Distance Education*, 3(2), 57-66, 1989.

Doulai, P. and Mandel, M., "Computer and Information Literacy Skills for Professional Engineering Educators", In *the Proceedings of Australasian Universities Power Engineering Conference*, Melbourne, 1996.

Khanna S.K., "Challenges of Higher Technical Education in India", *Convocation Address*, DCE, Sept. 1993.

Kirby, E., "Building Interaction in Online and Distance Education Courses", *Paper presented at the Society for Information Technology and Teacher Education International Conference,* 10th, San Antonio, TX, February, 1999.

Kraft. P and Truex D., "Postmodern Management and Information Technology in the Modern Industrial Corporation" R. Baskerville, S. Smithson, O. Ngwenyama and J.I DeGross (eds.) *Transforming Organisations with Information Technology IFIP*, 1994.

Paterson K. G. "Student Perceptions of Internet-Based Learning Tools in Environment Engineering Education", *Journal of Engineering Education*, 88:3, pp. 295-304, 1999.

Portway, P., and Lane, C., *Technical Guide to Teleconferencing and Distance Learning*. San Ramon, CA: Applied Business telecommunications, 1992.

Reid, K. A., *Impact of Technology on learning effectiveness. AT&T CEDL Newsletter*, 1995.

Tapscott, D., *Growing up Digital: The Rise of the Net Generation*. New York: McGraw-Hill Book Company, 1998.

Zigerell, J., *The Users of Television in American Higher Education*, New York: Praeger, 1991.

8

Globalisation of Teacher Training

We have entered into a period of competitive environment of globalisation, which requires us to develop our potential for capturing new markets and retaining old markets and for improving our overall productivity. This requires very competent professional young managers having at least a nodding acquaintance with functional areas of management. The technological prises, public systems and even on our large cities change sweeping the world would have a pronounced impact on the emerging society.

The growth that is seen in service industries and the way they are overtaking manufacturing industries in the post-industrial world are a pointer to the changes that are bound to take place. There would be a major change in the quality and composition of the labour force, with considerable shift towards knowledge-workers as opposed to blue-collar workers. Another change that one could expect, is the increasing liberalisation in the industrial and fiscal policies within the country. This would result in the private sector moving on to a position of parity with the public sector and providing competition to it, resulting in increased efficiency and better quality products. The increased liberalisation is expected to provide a boost to industrial activity itself.

The increased power and managerial capabilities of industries would make us at least equal to the second level of game players in the international field with reasonably good competitive capabilities. This indicates globalisation of economies, which would be reflected in freer movements of capital, technology, professional manpower and products. The multinational corporations, which are already in India or the ones which would move to India, would increasingly be convinced of the competence of our technical and managerial manpower.

The increasing concern for efficiency, accountability and better performance on the part of all public institutions and industries would have its impact on the performance of public sector enterprises, public systems and even on our large cities and municipal cooperations.

The share of international trade in the GNP of our country is increased. As the growth and success of a nation depends considerably on its performance in the international market, this phenomenon will become true in our case too. With the kind of highly educated and professional manpower that we have, supported by the thousands of trained technicians that we produce every year, we should be able to move into international markets with greater confidence.

There are all kinds of institutions claiming all sorts of spurious foreign tie-ups with foreign institutions and trying to attract students taking advantage of the craze for everything foreign, and sometimes even promising foreign degrees. Management education did start with foreign collaboration. The Management Studies Department of Delhi had received substantial inputs from foreign universities, especially from the USA.

Management education in India can be said to have developed its own strong foundations, yet globalisation has become an irreversible phenomenon and no country can really stay aloof from it. There is thus need for continuous upgradation of curriculum and also reorienting the management faculty to meet the requirements of globalisation, to prepare global mangers.

The curricula in our institutions are still very old-fashioned, concentrating on behavioural sciences, classical theories of business and quantitative techniques of the fifties and the sixties. They do not take into account the knowledge of the new information technology and its tremendous impact on organisation and management; the problems and issues facing transborder business operations or global business operations and all the organisational and managerial implications that follow; and the need for cross-cultural communication.

MBAs rarely enter into the niche areas of business and pioneering services to become successful entrepreneurs. And liberalisation has brought in a host of multinationals which are infusing different work culture. As compared to engineers who traditionally took to entrepreneurship in the past, the MBAs are better equipped. Studies at IIMC have revealed that technocrat entrepreneurs are wedded to their products, with a false notion that their products will automatically sell in the market.

The major shortcoming in area of management education of are given below.

i) Management education has become highly techniques-oriented. It is necessary for it to become behaviour-oriented for effective utilisation of human source.
ii) Management education has become job oriented, it should become entrepreneurial oriented.
iii) There is inadequate attention to business ethics.
iv) There is specialisation in functional areas, but these are narrow lines.
v) There is inadequate attention to international dimensions of business activity.
vi) There is inadequate linkage between business houses and management institutes.
vii) Emphasis will have to be given on sectorial management and also on information technology.

Management students must develop reading habits to induce them to think independently with a deep insight into the conceptual basis of various issues in management practices. Students must buy original textbooks wherein a fundamental analysis is made of the practical side of management. They must also read biographies and autobiographies of great innovators, entrepreneurs and captains of industries. The bookshelf at the residence of every student must be adorned by classical books on management written by world class eminent thinkers.

Nowadays, the number of students aspiring and seeking foreign education is increasing. The multicultural approach to education is relatively new to most countries. Still time has come to realise its need so that ethnic clashes can be reduced in future to the minimum, and a better humane society is built.

There are two types of internationalisation of education. First is students from one country go to other countries to study, and second is foreign academic institutions work with/without local institutions to offer academic degrees of their own country.

In the first way, there are some latest trends in international mobility of students has taken place in the Indian context. During the year 1996-97, 6426 students went abroad—reaching the level of 1992-93 (6499). There was sharp decrease in numbers during 1993-94 (2284), 1994-95 (2983), and 1995 96(3478) 80 to 85 per cent of these students were male.

According to UNESCO report, there were 39,626 Indian students enrolled in different countries abroad during 1995. The number of Indian students going to America (USA/Canada) has decreased from almost 90 per cent in 1990-91 to 47 per cent in 1996-97. Number of those going to Europe have increased from 6.5 per cent to 22 per cent and to Australia and New Zealand, from mere 2.7 per cent to 27 per cent during the same period. Around 40 per cent students go abroad for engineering and technology, 25 per cent for management, 15 per cent for medicine and 20 per cent for other subjects. Break up between first degree, Master's degree and Ph.D programmes is not known. Merely two to three per cent students are funded by scholarships, balance are self-financed (30 per cent) or funded from unspecified sources (67 per cent).

Unspecified sources are presumed to be self-financed only Number of foreign students in India has decreased sharply from nearly 1300 in early nineties to 5901 during 1996-97. In total, there are 16 lakh foreign students enrolled for higher education in the 50 major host countries.

In the second way of academic internationalisation is that of foreign institutes working with local institutions or setting up shops of their own offering academic programmes and degree off the shelf or based on models from Europe, the United States or Australia. Distance education, using the internet, is beginning to be used to deliver degrees. Twinning arrangements in which a university in Asia links up with a Western institution, a common way of offering offshore degrees. Though internationalisation in higher education has been age-old, the current wave has a new aspect.

In the Asian context, a regional conference was organised by the UNESCO in Japan to work out national strategies and regional cooperation on higher education for the 21st century. The conference recognised the diversity and variety of higher education systems across the region which makes generalisations difficult but adds tremendous opportunities for interaction and learning through the sharing of experience.

The various current higher education systems of the region have been built on different local traditions of scholarship and learning. They have also looked to a variety of European countries and the United States for models for modern university development. They have adopted and combined the features of different models to suit the local needs. Some such as those of the Indian subcontinent are still largely public systems, whereas in Japan, Thailand, Korea and the Philippines a high proportion of students are enrolled in private higher education institutions.

MULTICULTURALISM IN EDUCATION

Multiculturalism include cultural retention, creative encounters, and interchange and overcoming cultural barriers to foster a society in which people and groups of all cultures are accepted. It promotes human and group relations in which ethnic, racial, religious, and linguistic similarities and differences are valued and accepted.

The goal of multicultural education is definitely that of creating an aware citizen with a global view of life so that he believes in and promotes an appreciation for cultural diversity, social equality racial harmony and national cohesiveness, which are basic to a democratic society. A multicultural society can only work in a climate of tolerance. The responsibility for overcoming intolerance should be borne equally by the teachers, administrators, parents, and the society at large.

There is a need to return to a system of education that would stress human valued, an education for life as well as for jobs, and the policy of multiculturalism in education/ multicultural education/intercultural education/humanistic education/ liberal arts education is an answer to this. Multicultural education is preparation for the social, political and economic realities that individuals experience in culturally diverse and complex human encounters. These realities have both national and international dimensions. This preparation provides a process by which an individual develops competencies for perceiving, believing, evaluating, and behaving in different cultural settings. There are four major reasons for the teaching of multicultural education. They are:

i) An appreciation of multiculturalism is required to eliminate racism, ethnic discrimination and racial prejudice;
ii) An understanding and appreciation of other cultures and an awareness of the arts, music, languages and customs

of others can only serve to enhance and improve the quality of life for all.

iii) Multicultural education is the key to the creation of harmony and peace which begins at home and spreads across the globe, through international understanding and cooperation; and

iv) The myth that multicultural education is something needed to be done only in social studies classes, is to be dispelled.

The rationale for interest in multicultural education emerged in the Indian context due to the eruption of some extremely violent communal riots. The country has always been proud of its unity despite diversity. But the occurrences of such riots shake the very foundations of democracy. One of the cures may be education of the young and re-education of the adults about the similarities of different groups and they are taught to value the differences.

Teachers must have access to specialist assistance. All the classifications of teachers are vital to the process of education. It is not appropriate to consider only the classroom teacher. Others are vital elements of the support system. Classroom teachers can be taken as the first line managers, others as coaches and as general managers. Any policy relating to education can bring desired results only if all of them work together as a team.

Social and technological changes pose a substantial ongoing challenge to teachers. The technology of modern communications greatly influences all our students. Social and cultural changes too are significant. To take care of increasing cultural diversity, teachers must have the awareness of multiculturalism implies the concept of life and identity in which people and groups of all cultures are accepted as equals. It implies the freedom of all individuals and groups to the retention and development of their cultures as a part of the nation's identity.

Teachers are in an unquestioned position to contribute positively to the development of muticultural and intercultural understanding. The major challenge to teachers and other educators today is the challenge to change and innovate. One such challenge is multicultural education. However, a challenge is an opportunity. Therefore, multiculturalism should be taken as an opportunity to look beyond national boundaries to take benefit of technological changes taking place globally.

Due to fast technological advancement in communications and transportation, the world is becoming smaller every day making multiculturalism a necessity. At the UNESCO conference emerged a new appreciation of the role of higher education in technological and economic development and in providing specialised professionals. There was a strong consensus about the importance of continuing education for all professionals and for a more thorough commitment to the concept and practice of lifelong learning.

One area where universities were concluded to be making a major contribution to other sectors was the direct involvement in the training of school teachers and staff development activities for teachers. Strengthening the quality of teaching in schools will lead to better prepared university students. It was also observed that teachers, professors, and technical and administrative staff must be given trading that enabled them to integrate new information and technologies into their teaching programmes.

In order to enable teachers to play a crucial role in the implementation of a policy on intercultural education, they need to be trained. In general, for a teachers training programme, the following framework may be followed:

i) Culture and cultural pluralism. It includes:
   a) reality of culture
   b) diversity and particularity of cultures
   c) relativity of cultures
   d) dynamics of culture.

ii) Communication and cultural barriers
   a) theories of communication
   b) culture and diversity of mode of perception
   c) body language and non-verbal communication
   d) languages and diversity of ways of thinking according to cultures.

iii) Psychological identity and inter-ethnic relations
   a) cultural differences and question of psychological identity
   b) racism and discrimination
   c) stereotypes
   d) intercultural understanding and minority situations: sociopolitical aspects
   e) bureaucracy, cultures, and social classes.

There are three main approaches that can adopted in relation to multicultural management in education. They are:

i) *Ethnic specific approach:* This approach is supported by such group that are particularly interested in cultural retention. The purpose is to preserve, maintain and to provide for the continued development of a given culture. The ethnic group usually takes the lead in organising ethnic schools, which teach the language, values, and other important cultural attributes. The education provided promotes the socialisation of children within the culture. It promotes in-group/ out-group differentiation and group maintenance.

ii) *Problem-oriented approach:* This approach is a form of multicultural education usually stresses inter-cultural understanding and group relations.

iii) *Cultural-intercultural approach:* This approach differs from the second approach in terms of cohesiveness, duration, clientele, and motive or objective.

The third approach can be said to be the best out of the three approaches. Involvement of communities, groups, teachers, administrators, students, parents as well as of educational societies and trusts is important to promote this kind of education. Therefore, the development, implementation, and evaluation of multicultural or intercultural education must be a partnership. To integrate multiculturalism into the curriculum, a process of curricular reform is required as that has some benefits over add-ons approach.

Research evidence confirms that the 70 or 80 hour multicultural experimental treatment is not usually effective. While all pervasive approach may not yield miraculous results, it can be seen as more effective because it is compatible with the ongoing process of attitude formation and modification. The integrative approach produces a reformed curriculum, which is in harmony with the life experiences of students who have a strong identification and involvement with their ethnic communities. Multiculturalism should be seen as a vehicle for reflecting and promoting social justice.

When judged by its success, multicultural education will be measured by the increased attention to human relations, group development, language teaching, teacher awareness and sensitivity administration adjustments, student interests and concerns, community involvement, unity and equal opportunity for all. Implementing programmes, which foster the concept of education that is multicultural, is a formidable task. But the potential of a more humane and understanding people, cognisant of and enriched by their various cultural heritage, yet sustained and strengthened by their commitment to ensuring the human rights of all, should be more than worth the effect.

Multiculturalism indicates cultural liberty is a lively social relation between many open systems, a synthesis of new culture out of many social traditions which is never finished and which is modified and renewed by every fresh wave of immigration. It is not a political device to slow down a process of assimilation to a dominant culture but a common pursuit in which every tradition contributes to community. It goes beyond the individual liberty on which every democratic state rests to a liberty of groups, families and persons to be themselves.

INTERNATIONALISTION OF HIGHER EDUCATION

The higher education system today is more complex than ever before. The role of teachers has been redefined. Physical distances and places are no more important with new information technologies. Virtual libraries are substituting traditional libraries; classroom teaching is being substituted by web browsing. Traditional approach to develop curriculum based on perceived requirements at a given level has been replaced by the requirements of skills and professions and therefore curricula and study programmes have become more flexible, dynamic and complex. Boundaries between natural and social sciences have become irrelevant.

Universities and other institutions of higher education is taking on new features which of course require new modes of management. As universities evolve and grow in complexity, management has become highly professionalised and new management techniques have developed. The design, flow and accessibility of the information needed for management decision-making requires skills and systems that are distant from the traditional ones.

Internationalisation of higher education is the process of integrating an international/intercultural dimension into the teaching, research and service functions of the institution. Care needs to be taken that neither political nor economic rationale dominate internationalisation. It is important to note that links between international and intercultural factors are very strong.

Initially most of the countries have economic motives for internationalisation with exceptions like Sweden where an initial national policy was established as early as 1970s. The educational rationale for internationatisation, which considers international cooperation as indispensable for maintaining the quality of higher education and research, is still supported by most countries.

However, the economic rationale of international competitiveness and long-term or direct economic benefits is becoming increasingly important. This in particular is demonstrated in countries where the recruitment of foreign students has become a strong priority in the national policy.

Although there is diversity between countries, there seems to be a trend from internationalisation as an investment or input into the higher education system, towards internationalisation as an expected performance or output of the system. Besides, other goals such as solidarity in relation to developing countries, humanitarian and peacekeeping related aims are also factors shaping internationalisation policies.

Internationalisation seems as if the attempt is to go in the direction of universal learning and universal higher education system in the context of a new modern world and a new age, the information age, in which society, economy and knowledge are part of a global environment, a mix of local and global influences. Earlier the chief value of education lay to serve the administrative and economic needs of the nation-states and became an essential aspect of the development of national identity. Today learning again has become international. There is a strong emphasis on international cooperation and exchange. Institutions are developing their own strategies to internationalise their research and their teaching.

Knight and Wit had distinguished four groups of rationales for internationalisation in higher education: academic, social/ cultural, political and economic. Rationales can be described as motivations for integrating an international dimension into higher education. While analysing rationales, the diversity of stakeholders' groups in higher education: the government sector, the private sector and the educational sector need to be taken into account. In education sector distinction needs to be made between three subgroups—the institutional level, the academics and their departments, and the students. Different countries place different emphasis on these rationales with a different priority.

Academic and social/cultural rationales played an important role in developing internationalisation policies. Although, no more dominant, these are important in shaping the contemporary higher education systems. Internationalisation brings global environment on more equal terms, higher education and society can move away from dependency syndrome of nations who took initial advantage of internationalisation processes. Many national leaders have had their education abroad, and, in that other cultural environment, became more attached to their own national identity than before.

With the passage of time and with the growth of nations, political rationales became more and more important. The political rationale been dominant in post-Second World War initiatives to internationalise higher education. But after the end of the col war, the emphasis has changed from the political to the economic.

The economic rationale is expressed in several ways, such as:

i) the emphasis on internationalisation because of the requirements of the modern, more global labour force needs;
ii) joint international research and development projects to compete internationally in new technology; and
iii) more attention to marketing of higher education on the international market.

Such economic rationales for internationalisation have an impact on the local context. For instance, in business education, international business seems to become the main curriculum of business schools, responding to this supposed need for an international labour force. That, even in a more and more global economy, the large majority of the labour force will still be working in a local context, tends to become sometimes forgotten.

In the emphasis on research and development, research oriented to social, cultural and local issues is in danger to get less priority and opportunity And the growing competition for international students may have a negative impact both on the quality of the education—by lower selection standards—and on the basic finance of higher education institutions for the training of local students, as institutions are more and more based on funding resulting from recruitment of foreign students, that has to take place on a vulnerable international market.

The economic rationales that push at present institutions of higher education to become more international are mainly external factors. That does not mean that universities have no incentive from inside to become more international. The academic environment itself has changed radically in the past 50 years.

Higher education has become more deregulated, diverse in income sources, privatised and market oriented. The entrepreneurial university of these days again feels an inside need to become more international. The academic rationale, in addition to the traditional search for universal knowledge and understanding, has become more modern. More emphasis on professional education, on continuous education, on new areas such as environmental studies, information science etc., require a comparative and international dimension, coming from outside, but also from demands of faculty and students.

Generally, there are four sets of motivation factors for internationalisation. These are political, economic, educational and cultural. Importance of and interrelation between these keep on changing depending on specific situations.

i) *Political factors*: Political factors may include: fostering understanding for world peace. They influencing future decision-makers/opinion formers, and raising the international profile of a country abroad.

ii) *Economic factors*: Economic factors for internationalisation may include income from foreign students. These securing funds from international organisations, building economic competitivity, and fitting students for a global job market.

iii) *Education motivation*: Education motivation for internationalisation may include institution and capacity building. They enabling researchers in specialised fields to make advances in line with their peers, providing access to teaching, research or services of the highest quality regardless of national origin, offering home students contact with other systems through foreign students, being taught by teachers with international experience or following international curricula, and raising the quality of the home system by the application of international standards.

iv) *Cultural rationale:* The cultural rationale could include: fulfilling the cultural function of the institution; most universities consider themselves to be international, development of the individual, and fostering knowledge and appreciation of own culture especially language in other countries.

A clear trend in various countries concerns the shift towards wider international cooperation. Their focus is especially placed on economically dynamic countries in Southeast Asia and, to a certain extent also in Latin America. National policies for internationalisation are still predominantly based on the traditional instruments of mobility of students.

However, in some countries a shift can be observed from the individual to the institutional level. National policies include an increasingly wider range of activities and focus more strongly on curriculum, institutional organisation and management and on structure of the higher education system as such. Conceptual disconnection between internationalisation policies and general higher education policy is also evident in many countries.

The development towards more comprehensive policies can be considered as positive in view of sustainable changes taking place in various spheres of education. The initial narrow definition of internationalisation in terms of international academic mobility seems to be widening. This contributes to diminishing the conceptual disconnection between internationalisation and higher education policy in general. Development of internationalisation policies are being governed by enhanced influence of institutional and market forces.

A trend towards decentralisation and increased institutional autonomy can be observed. In some cases funding is consequently being integrated into the institutional budget or is being awarded as a lump sum. More extreme examples of completely market-driven models, where the role of the national authorities is limited to creating conditions, may be found in case of the United Kingdom and Australia. Although national policies may become more institutionally oriented, comprehensive and more coherently planned, funding for internationalisation is often still individually oriented and fragmented, measures for evaluation and quality assurance of internationalisation are generally still lacking. Besides the increased international mobility of students, teachers and researchers, and the establishment of numerous international contacts and networks, national policies have resulted in changes in regulation and legislation on higher education.

Examples concern the recognition of foreign credentials, the possibility of teaching in other languages, the country's system for academic degrees, fee policies, or transferability of students grants. These changes have increased the institutional autonomy and the freedom to develop international programmes. In smaller countries relatively more and more rapid effects in terms of changes at the system level can be observed.

Effects at the institutional level include the establishment of an infrastructure for internationalisation, including the creation of a range of new positions, the development of strategies for internationalisation and of international study programmes, and an increased use of non-national languages as medium of instruction. In a large number of countries policies are being affected by various international forces. International policies are only one of these forces. Besides, international market forces play a role. The influence of this factor is especially demonstrated in countries that expect direct economic benefits from internationalising the higher education system.

In Australia, internationalisation of higher education may be traced to the post-world war era which saw significant changes in the foreign policies of many developed nations. These reflected their response to the end colonialism, emergence of independent developing nations, growing international relations and world trade, and desire to promote good will through support to developing nations in various spheres of development.

Consequently when Colombo plan was launched in 1951, Australia was a key partner. This was the first step in the direction of internationalisation which saw the entry of the Australian government in the sponsorship of international students to study in Australian institutions. The period that followed saw a significant increase in number of overseas students in the category of sponsors and private.

Private students were treated on par with the Australian students. Their entry was primarily controlled by the immigration policies which were subjected to change from time to time. The major policy shift took place in the mid-1980s with the release of two major reports—the committee to review the Australian Overseas Aid Programme Known as Jackson

Report and the Committee on Review of Private Overseas Student Policy known as the Goldring Report.

The government went ahead with the recommendations of the Jackson report and announced a new Overseas Student Policy in 1985 which paved the way for the enrolment of overseas students other than subsidised students. These students were required to satisfy entry requirements as well as were to pay to total cost of the course. This was followed by Policy on the Export of the Education Services which was to facilitate recruitment of full fee paying students. This paved the way for greater enrolment of overseas students. Institutions had to satisfy that enrolment of overseas students did not lead to displacement of Australian students.

In 1989 announced that from 1990, there would be no more subsidised students. The government also announced the federal government funding will be based on number of domestic students. This had serious implications for those institutions which had a large number of subsidised students as it meant that they will have to enrol the same number of full fee paying students to maintain the same level of financing. In order to make sure that this new policy initiative did not create much damage, the government announced some targeted scholarship schemes. While emphasis on recruitment of full fee paying overseas students provided commercial benefits to Australia, it also provided many other benefits.

This was well endorsed by government in 1992 during refocusing on international education. This refocusing, expressed by the then Minister for Employment, Education and Training involved a move away from a concentration on exporting student places to a recognition of the wider activities integrally involved in international education and the wide, sometimes indirect, benefits, which flow from seeking to internationalise our education system.

The Australian government recognises that international education is an increasingly important part of Australia's international relations. It uniquely spans the cultural, economic, and interpersonal dimensions of international relations. It assists cultural understanding for all parties involved. It enriches Australia's education and training systems and the wider Australian society by encouraging a more international outlook.

The new policy had a focus on Asia Pacific region and widened scope to include research, student and faculty exchange and collaborations. All these initiatives culminated in the Statement of Purpose made by the Higher Education Council of the National Board of Employment, Education and Training in 1992. The Ministerial statement of 1992 followed by the statement by the National Board of Employment, Education and Training led to the emergence of a new perspective for internationalisation of education.

This new perspective was distant away from its focus on trade and incorporated new elements of explosion of knowledge, international and intercultural relations within the framework of the policy of multiculturalism. This led to significant increase in full fee paying overseas students in Australia. According to the latest available data 1,47,000 international students were studying in Australian institutions.

Countries carefully observe the developments in higher education in other countries and that these observations, or direct inquiries, form more and more often an input into the process of developing new national policies for higher education. International market forces and enhanced institutional autonomy play an increasingly important role in the formulation of internationalisation policies and in the directions that higher education policies might take more generally.

PARADIGM TOWARDS QUALITY TEACHER EDUCATION

The evolution of distance education methodology has changed

the entire concepts of traditional education. In India, the idea of distance education was mooted way back in early sixties, that is hardly fifteen years after the independence to cope up with the pressure of the ever-growing demand of higher education which could not be met by the conventional system. Distance education is often distinguished from correspondence study by the notion of three way teaching. It can be equated with the combined, systematic and flexible use of at least three major elements: print-based communication, broadcasting and face-to-face contact in support of an independent learner.

The growing awareness that learning, not teaching is the decisive factor in education, has brought support to distance education along with other methods of independent study. The physical separation of teacher and learner envisages a different role for the teacher. He may meet the students only for 'selected tasks' such as counselling, giving tutorials or seminars or solving study problems. The idea of having correspondence institutions was that one can handle the problem arising out of the infrastructural limitations by not calling the learners to the academic institutions, but by sending the learning materials to the residence of the learners. The teacher plays a very dominant role in the overall transactions of teaching and learning. We develop interest in a particular subject because we were introduced to the same by a competent teacher.

Today, 'globalisation' and 'liberalisation of economy' has been affecting every sphere of our life and higher education is no exception. It is because of this we are now having multinationalisation of education. Internet has opened the facilities for web-based training. Today everyone faces an overwhelming challenge for increasing efficiency, effectiveness and competitiveness. For this, we need access to different vistas of knowledge which, is not possible through the conventional mode of teaching. We need to have a fundamental change in the mode of training being imparted to the learners. These changes are creating metamorphosis within the institutions of learning to find new ways to educate and keep students update. Delivering training via internet is a key tool to meet all these requirements and virtual classroom or virtual campus is a consequence of this—web-based training.

Through a dedicated network of computers we can bring in teachers live from different locations. We may also have interactions with the teachers through this mode. The multimedia has immense possibilities as regards bringing live not only the audio aspect of the teachers' deliberations but visual aspects also. On the visual display unit of the computer we may arrange for bringing in the teacher with his body language in one point and in another portion we can have some demonstration. The structured component of the learning package is very well disseminated through computer networks.

The process of development of mankind has occurred via the development of three sectors—agricultural, industrial and Information Technology. The requirement of land or brick and mortar infrastructure is virtually nil for the information technology revolution. We only have our good old earth with us and with the passage of time we shall have to accept the reality that real estate will become scarcely available and that also against huge costs. We need to use to our advantage the most important virtue of the information technology revolution that no additional real estate will be necessary.

The academic institutions can very well manage IT-based education with whatever brick and mortar infrastructure they have. A proper media policy can only help in reducing the rural-urban gap as regards information technology resources. However, the onus is also on the common man to break the traditional inertia in this regard. When we can make use of technology in our household activities, we can also make use of the same for dissemination of education. The distance teaching institutions depend heavily on the conventional counterparts as they form their resources for providing experts and most importantly the infrastructural facilities for providing learner support services. So, the growth chart of distance teaching institutions need not be a cause for concern. The conventional and the distance teaching institutions need to work in a tandem to increase, the outreach of education.

The contemporary model of teacher education though has grown manifold over the decades but over shadowed with severe criticism for being static and unresponsive to the emerging challenges of the present time. There is a growing feeling that teacher education is not effective in turning out efficient teachers and this concern is adequately reflected in the National Policy of Education (1986) and programme of Action (1992). The knowledge, skills and methodologies propagated by the system remain alien and never get assimilated to the school system.

Teacher education continued to be viewed in isolation, disconnected from other factors that shape the role and performance of teacher—recruitment, salary, working conditions and overall professional development. Over the years, few initiatives have taken place in the area of teacher education to translate policy rhetoric to practice, reflecting marginal implication on quality teacher education. In this context, importance of quality of teachers in improving the quality of education is far beyond question.

As a sequel to National Policy on Education and POA, a number of planned initiatives have been launched by establishment of District Institutes of Education (DIETs) and strengthening of teacher training institutions to IASEs and CTEs to provide both quality preservice and in-service education to teachers. The establishment of National Council of Teacher Education (NCTE) and its curriculum framework has been welcomed as a dynamic step in moving towards quality teacher education. As a major initiative, a competency based and commitment oriented curriculum for quality teacher education has been developed on a collaborative effort.

The scope of suggestive curriculum framework (1998) of teacher education has been developed keeping in view the country's need for different kinds of teachers to manage its educational system with efficiency and professionalism. Abroad curriculum frame work has been spelt out for different stages of school education. The framework has also suggested increase in the duration of B.Ed. programme to ensure professionalism in teacher education and provide a strong base for pursuing M.Ed. Programmes. It further presupposed that the duration will suitably be adjusted with the entry qualifications to bridge the mismatch between the needs of teacher education institutions and professional preparation of teacher educators working in such institutions. Besides this, some of the innovations in teacher education have been carried out by introducing 4 years integrated teacher education programme (B.A., B.Ed./B.Sc., B.Ed.) and M.Sc. Ed. programme (for the teachers at +2 stage). The programme has been developed on the premise that pedagogy for a subject should form an integral part of its content. Apart from this, some universities have attempted to introduce degree courses leading to primary teacher training.

Teachers for special education, for work education, higher education, non-formal and adult education and teachers working in other professional sectors of education have been occupying their due places in the broad domain of teacher education. All these efforts are aimed at translating the policy into effective practice for qualitative improvement in the teacher education system. It is clear that mere curriculum revision by NCTE will not suffice to improve the quality of training in the country. Nor will be establishment of institutional facilities such as DIETs, BRCs and CRCs be able to address the problems faced by the teacher training—both preservice and in-service. However, reforms attempted over the last few years have aimed at introducing improvement rather than restructuring the over all teacher education model.

The teacher education is needed to remain effective and functional to cope with changes occurring in quick succession in school and society and challenges to be faced in the new millennium. The building of 'new education' and 'the new teacher role'calls for integral and urgent measures directed towards expanded role of teachers necessitating the change in teacher education structure, design and curriculum. International Commission on education (1996) stressed the need for:

— attracting to the teaching profession more talented and adequately, academically prepared persons, and
— motivation and awareness for continuous upgradation of one's academic and professional competencies.

In India, the structure of school curriculum comprises four levels i.e., pre-primary, primary (I-V), upper primary (VI-VII), secondary (VIII-X), and senior Secondary (XI-XII). The existing system of teacher education has no synchronisation with sub stages of school education. It has been observed that teachers possessing qualifications like BTC/JBT/CT/DEd are eligible for teaching classes I-V and in some cases eligible for teaching classes at upper primary level (VI-VII). On the other hand B.Ed. degree holder are also eligible for teaching classes from VI-XII i.e. upper primary level to senior secondary stage. Hence, to teach at upper primary level both elementary and secondary teachers are eligible causing much anomalies and raising questions of teachers' ability to negotiate curriculum in relation to their differential qualification and training inputs.

The recent development in school curriculum has made it difficult for teachers with senior secondary qualification to teach subjects like math, science at classes VI-VIII. Even at the secondary stage, graduates find difficult to teach classes IX and X which demand subject specific teaching. Hence, a structural change is required in the contemporary model of teacher education so that it synchronises with sub stages of school education. With the transformation of the Elementary Teacher Training Institution (ETIs) to DIETs, it would be in the fitness of things to develop one programme for the elementary stage classes I-VI-VIII. The secondary teacher education should also have one programme (IX-XIII) wherein senior secondary teacher preparation programme can be subsumed. Hence, the structural change in teacher education requires only two programmes.

The present teacher education system is based on the assumption that lower academic qualification is required to teach at lower level of education i.e. elementary level. Hence varying level of entry qualifications are prescribed for teacher education programme for different stages of school education. The elementary teacher education programmes in different states require matriculation or higher secondary (+2) pass as the entry qualification. DIETs have prescribed senior secondary (Arts, Science and Commerce) as the desired qualification for admission to the preservice teacher education course offered by them. In case of secondary teacher education, the admission requirements is uniformly bachelor's degree in Arts, Science and Commerce. Integrated courses of 4 years duration for preparing secondary teachers is also in existence in Regional Institutes of Education (NCERT). The teachers with postgraduate qualifications along with B.Ed. are eligible to teach at +2 stage which has been integrated with the existing school system after the implementation of 10+2+3 pattern of education. However, the ever increasing amount of knowledge and information on the one hand and changing school curriculum on the other will require teachers with higher level of competencies.

The present trend envisages a positive direction as most of the entrants for elementary and secondary teacher education programmes are graduates and postgraduates respectively. The assumption regarding lower qualification at lower level was the guiding principle decade back keeping in view the then prevalent low enrolment and shortage of teachers and their inadequate work load. However, this assumption no longer holds true in the present time. A number of studies on need assessment have shown the content knowledge deficiencies of teacher teaching at primary stage.

The class teaching at the primary stage does not make primary teachers of varied backgrounds, confident to transact different subjects with same level of confidence. The teacher may face problems depending on their academic background of science or humanities. Accordingly, the system of class teaching in primary schools expects a teacher trainee to undergo training in all curricular areas. However, it appears difficult for a teacher of arts background to teach subjects like science and math at classes VI-VIII level and non-scholastic areas like art, music and dance which under present circumstances require professional training. At the secondary stage, a teacher is called upon to teach two subjects depending on his/her background. But the present school curriculum requirement of subject specialisation like physics, chemistry mathematics, language, geography, history, economics and a postgraduation qualification in the concerned subject appears to be essential keeping in view the present day realities in school education.

The organisation of curriculum for both elementary and secondary teacher education is much similar in their theoretical perspectives. However, the content of various courses at the secondary stage is slightly at a higher level in terms of number of syllabus components on the one hand and comprehensiveness on the other. A very conspicuous difference is in the number of teaching subjects a trainee has to offer. An elementary teacher trainee under practice teaching teaches all subjects at primary stage (class IV) and one or two subjects at the upper primary stage (VI-VIII). A secondary teacher trainee teaches two subjects of his/her specialisation from class VI to X but she/he might not have studied a subject at the graduation level. Thus, two points can be noted to suggest alternative paradigm i.e. overlapping of practice teaching at upper primary (VI-VII) level and efficiency to negotiate a subject not studied at the graduation level. Hence, supporting the argument of structural change, enhanced entry qualifications and subject teaching, the practice teaching should be confined to two subjects at the elementary teacher education programme and one subject at the secondary teacher training level.

Though establishment of DIETs have brought uniformity in the duration (2 years) in the elementary teacher education programme, yet some states follow elementary teacher training of different duration resulting in a lot of adhocism. The duration of ongoing teacher preparation at secondary stage is of one year. The secondary teacher education programme, leading to B.Ed degree, has multiple scope in our country as it requires a person to teach at elementary, secondary and senior secondary level. Integrated courses of longer duration have been planned and offered in some universities. The four year integrated teacher education programme leading to a combined degree of B.Sc., B.Ed has been running successfully in the four Regional Institutes of Education.

In the recent past, a few more institutions have started integrated programme. There are studies to indicate that the products of these integrated programmes are superior to the products of one year teacher education programme. The difference in effectiveness is attributed to several factors which include selection of meritorious students, programmed duration, integrated curriculum allowing simultaneous teaching of content and methods of teaching. Unfortunately, the experiment having the potential of professionalising the teaching profession has not been extensively implemented inspite of unambiguous support from several commissions and committees. Recent initiative of NCTE in extending duration of B.Ed from one year to two years in selected institutions has translated long felt need and demand of teacher educators, educationists and recommendations of commissions and committees to inculcate professionalism in teacher education programme. In years to come, the credibility of teacher education institutions will depend upon the rigour and richness of the programme they conduct and the research based on which these programme are planned, developed and implemented.

During the past few decades, organisation of teacher education programme has been institution based, but today distance mode has taken a prominent place. It has its genesis on the summer course leading to B.Ed. degree offered in the RIEs of NCERT. Gradual commercialisation and introduction of correspondence courses have raised a question with regard to the validity of distance mode as a strategy of professional preparation. On the other hand distance education is acknowledged worldwide as a valid strategy for professional education.

It is often stated that open learning and distance education is likely to prove as effective as the institution based training provided the programme is conducted with due rigour using multi mode approach. The provision of self learning, followed by frequent contact programmes at the accredited institutions and periodic teleconferencing shall go a long way in enhancing the quality of any professional preparation programme. In a broader perspective, component of distance education must find place in the traditional face to face mode in the form of multi channel mode—self learning materials, teleconferencing to bring rigour and professionalism in teacher preparation.

Hence, distance mode may be viewed in/a wider perspective and included both in preservice and in-service teacher preparation which can widen the horizon of teacher preparation to cope with the demand of self learning and life long education. The distance mode can very well be integrated with the traditional face to face mode of teacher preparation with constructive efforts and meticulous planning.

India is one of the very few countries where primary teacher training is not at the university level which has indirectly an adverse effect on the economic and social status of the teacher. This in turn affects the teachers, pride in the profession and consequently their performance. In educationally advanced countries, the entire teacher education system is a part of university system and is characterised, by equal rigour and prestige like other disciplines. As the university degree has much respectability and status in our society teacher education of all levels may form part of the university system to enhance the status of teaching profession and to improve quality of teacher education. The genesis of teacher education is multi-disciplinary which as part of higher education system may find its rightful place by embracing inputs from all disciplines. Inclusion of all institutions of teacher preparation as part of university system can bring rigour, quality, qualified entrants, qualified teacher educators to enhance the status of teaching force of our country. Thus the alternative paradigm matrix towards quality teacher education comprises:

i) Structural change
ii) Enhancing entry qualifications
iii) Shift from class teacher to subject teacher
iv) Shift in curriculum and practice teaching
v) Shift in programme duration
vi) Shift in mode of teacher preparation
vii) Shift in institutional arrangement
viii) Translating paradigm into action

Teacher education can not transcend teaching practice. So that, for quality improvement in teacher education it is imperative that teacher education should act in partnership with families, industry, business, voluntary agencies, people active in cultural life and teacher organisations. Academic and social issues are interrelated and interdependent. In contemporary context, any change visualised in the sphere of teacher education needs collaborative efforts from all. The school, community, the teacher training institutions and university system have to move collaboratively towards building a shared commitment for paradigm shift in teacher education.

To ensure effective and efficient implementation of teacher education programme, collaboration and networking is essential, The NPE (1986) also visualises creation of net- working arrangements between institutions of teacher education and university departments of education. This is mutually beneficial to all stake holders and society at large. Organisation of teacher education programme has to be such that it builds local level partnership at the institutional level between the teacher training institutions and schools in the neighbour hood.

In the present day context, teacher education institutions need to keep in continuous touch with institutions of higher learning and peer institutions for effective transmission of -knowledge and upgradation. Quality teacher education looks for quality performance. Advances in education depend largely on the qualifications, ability of teaching staff in general and on the human, pedagogical and technical qualities of the individual teacher. Collaborative change must bridge the gap between needs for education and status of teachers.

REFERENCES

Bengu G. and W. Swart, A., "Computer-Aided Total Quality Approach to Manufacturing Education in Engineering", *IEEE Transactions on Education*, 39:3, pp. 415-427, 1996.

Brooksfield, S.D., *The Skillful Teacher: On Technique, Trust, and Responsiveness in the Classroom,* San Francisco, CA: Jossey-Bass, 1990.

Kirby, E., "Building Interaction in Online and Distance Education Courses", *Paper presented at the Society for Information Technology and Teacher Education International Conference,* 10th, San Antonio, TX, February, 1999.

Madhu Parhar, "Surfing Through Web—Exploring a New Educational Resource", *University News*, November, 20, 2000.

Martin, B. L., "Using Distance Education to Teach Instructional Design to Preservice Teachers", *Educational Technology*, Vol. XXXIV, No. 3, March 1994.

Powar, K.B., Quality Assurance in Higher Education, *University News*, November, 27, 2000.

Savitha Rastogi, "Training of Teachers in Higher Education fro Multicultural Teaching and Learning", *University News*, February , 28, 2000.

Sheel Nuna, "Internationalisation of Higher Education", *University News*, February 7, 2000.

9

Distance Education and Virtual Lessons

Developments in information technology has spawned a number of innovations in virtual education, or distance learning, where you learn at your own computer terminal from instructors who are physically located miles away. Distance learning offers numerous benefits to individuals, organisations, and even to society in general. For individuals, it provides access to education or training that they may not otherwise be able to pursue. For organisations it provides a cost efficient way to train or educate a large number of learners irrespective of their geographical location.

As individuals are offered more opportunities to learn, distance learning might end up being an avenue to increase the overall literacy in society through greater access to education. Doing a search on virtual education, or distance learning, on any internet search engine will give you a vast list of virtual education resources. While it is still in its infancy, virtual education is already making it possible for everyone from kindergarten students to business professionals to learn at their own pace, from the comfort of their own home.

Distance learning offers organisations can offer continuing training to their employees. It allows employees to take training courses without having to travel to education locations and without having to spend time away from their regular work environment. By providing easy access to high quality training to all of their employees, organisations can continue to increase the knowledge base of their organisation through individual learning.

Distance learning will not replace traditional education in the foreseeable future. It is a complement to the traditional learning environment. By using distance learning as an add-on to traditional classroom education or as a replacement for some courses, institutions can develop a richer overall learning environment available to a greater population base. Since web-based distance learning alternatives can be used as complements or replacements for traditional courses, every organisation involved with training or education can make use of web-based learning tools.

Distance learning reducing the IT labour shortage by providing greater access to individuals who want to receive education and training in technology fields when such training or education is not normally available to them. This includes individuals who have current careers and do not have time for scheduled classroom courses, or individuals who live in geographically remote areas where technology courses of the type they require are not available. Distance learning helps to reduce the digital divide by providing access to courses in remote areas or neighbourhoods where such courses would not be offered otherwise. For this to happen, however, communities must organise themselves to provide computer access to these neighbourhoods.

Organisations will benefit greatly from using distance learning when they have global operations since they can provide a consistent and standardised training for all of their employees worldwide. Distance education is the practical subset of education that deals with instruction in which distance and time are the criteria attributes; that is, student and teacher are separated by distance and/or time. Interactivity in instruction under these time and distance constraints is a variable that is likely to be critical to the success of distance education. Distance education suffers from a lack of theory.

The term 'interaction' has been misused and "carries so many meanings as to be almost useless unless specific submeanings can be defined and generally agreed upon." The general lack of theory in distance education of has been cited by numerous researchers in AECT&RISE's recent update of the distance education literature.

We will have more opportunities to learn through computers, with computers, and from computers. Generally, the focus of distance education has been on using the computer primarily as a communication tool. The "computer-as-mindtool" approach suggests that working with the computer in an authentic task acts as a stimulus for learning. Despite criticism of teacher-in-the box CBT, efforts to improve the humanness and adaptability of our interactions with computers will likely improve our ability to learn from them. We have only begun to gain the critical mass of interface technologies needed to make the computer an intelligent partner in instruction. Work in the development of intelligent agents attempts to produce software that acts as an intelligent assistant.

Some intelligent agents feature a conversational component that has a human visage and displays facial gestures—in essence, displaying personality or character. As we combine these capabilities with natural language understanding and the ability to process "spoken speech" the computer approaches the role of partner in a conversation, rather than a questioner or simple conditional decision maker. These streams converge on the need for a definition of interactivity, both in distance learning through computers as communication tools and in intelligent instructional systems where we learn from the computer tutor/teacher.

The intent of this article is to provide a structural definition of interactivity, with the goal of describing and delimiting a broad and general process. This structure suggest, additional variables that could likely be valuable in understanding interaction in instruction.

In creating a mathematical model of the communication process, concentrated on the structure of communication, and the properties of information itself, independent of the meaning of the communication. The information theory model has been valuable as a Rosetta stone for communication researchers in the areas of both human and machine communication. By forcing us to think about the structural aspects of communication, we have gained insight into both human and machine systems.

There are four major attributes to the concept of interactivity:

— Interactivity is a message loop.

— Instructional interactivity occurs from the learner's point of view and does not occur until a message loop from and back to the student has been completed.

— Instructional interactivity has two distinct classes of outputs: content learning and affective benefits.

— Messages in an interaction must be mutually coherent.

Interactivity is a message loop: Structurally, interactivity is a circuit of messages flowing from an originating entity to a target entity and then returning back to the originating entity. We shall refer to this as an interactive loop. Entities in an interactive loop can be students, instructors, computers, or others capable of receiving and sending messages. For example, common interactive loop patterns might be student to teacher to student, student 1 to student 2 and back to student 1, or student to computer programme to student. A completed message loop is shown below:

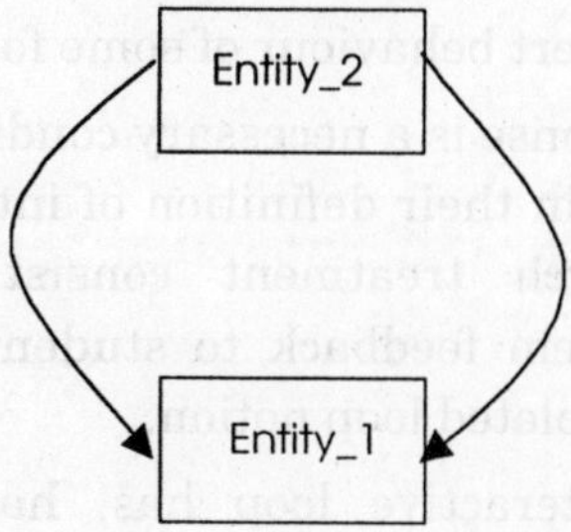

Figure 1: A completed message loop between two entities

This relatively powerful message cycle and used the term cybernetics to describe the loop. Communication and control in a cybernetics loop were essentially the same activity; an entity can control itself by feedback messages from the environment. "Thus the theory of control in engineering, whether human or animal or mechanical, is a chapter in the theory of the messages".

'Message' in an interactive loop refers not only to spoken messages but also to overt physical activities that are directly perceived by either entity. Contemporary authors use a similar concept in the area of systems dynamic modelling. The causal loop or feedback loop in system dynamics is claimed to be central in understanding human, organisational, and machine behaviour.

The causal loop represents the instrumental actions that one makes within a complex system, and their associated feedback chain. The notion of the causal loop concurs that control and communication both happen via messages passed between entities, forming a complete interactive loop. The operation of interaction as consisting of a physical response and feedback based on the response, hence describing a loop. However, their, definition also claims that "a physical response, by itself, is neither a necessary nor sufficient condition for interaction." It is not clear how one sends a message without overt behaviour of some form.

A physical response is a necessary condition of interaction. The loop structure in their definition of interactivity. A "fully interactive" research treatment consisting of embedded questions and system feedback to student responses, again supporting the completed loop notion.

A complete interactive loop has, happened when the teacher communicates a message to the student, and the student responds back to the teacher. However from a student point of view the loop is only half completed; the student has sent a message to the teacher, but often there is no response in return. In this case we have an open circuit. If we look at interactivity from the student perspective, we realise that many alleged interactive lessons and devices are not interactive at all. For example, a teacher may ask a student for a response, and receive the response from the student but fail to provide feedback, thus failing to complete the student's interactive loop. From the student perspective the student response is sent "into the vapour" with no sense of transmission received, transmission accepted, transmission understood, or transmission lost. Learning happens solely within the individual learner.

Although instruction may provide stimuli, the messages of interest flow from the student and back to the student in a student-entered loop. An interesting issue regarding the perception of interactivity occurs with branching computer-based training in which the instructional programme selects different paths based upon student responses. Such an interactive system may not appear to be interactive to the student;

because a student does not see the alternative branches, the programme may appear to be linear to the student. Even though the programme is responding the student may not sense that the system's displays are predicated on his or her message. Unless the student sees that he or she is skipping material, or being led to remedial material, the student may not actually perceive the computer's differential responses as interactive.

The "classroom lecture," may actually be more interactive then we acknowledge. Obviously, the straight "transmission" lecture has little opportunity for interactivity. However most lectures that we have witnessed are not delivered to that extreme. Generally a classroom instructor in the process of lecturing experts and encourages students to interrupt with questions. The possibility for student to ask a question of a teacher and receive a return message fulfils our definition of interactivity, in some cases better than so-called interactive technologies.

A student's perception of interaction is not necessarily correlated with the actual amount of time in interaction. A distance learning television classroom, where it was possible to measure the time of interaction. Interestingly, the students' perception of interactivity did not correlate with the actual clock time of interactions. This led the researchers to conclude that perceived interactivity is a psychological construct of each student. It is more likely that the interaction time as measured in their study was inflated by including messages that were not part of the student to teacher to student interaction. That is, their definition may have classified teacher-entered actions that we would not consider interactive by our emerging definition.

Therefore, their variable of perceived interaction may actually be closer to our definition of interaction. Apparently, students perceive interactivity as a student-entered event; large amounts of classroom activity may not correlate with a single student's individual interactivity.

Two distinct types of effects can occur through interactivity:

i) Content learning
ii) Affective benefits.

Content learning is herein described as purposeful learning directed toward attaining an instructional goal. Affective benefits are described as emotions and values toward instructional artifacts that are dampened or amplified. We find that content learning seems to be the better understood. A similar set of ideas were alternatively referred to as instructional interactivity and social interactivity. Although these terms seem to reflect the role of the interaction in the instructional process, rather than the effect of the interaction.

Content learning: Interaction with the environment is the basis for learning, is but one example of a learning theorist who explains the content learning effects of interactivity. Variations of behaviourism cite interaction with environment as reciprocal determinism that produces learned responses. Content learning from a cognitive perspective can be accounted for using schema theory, which posits that knowledge is organised in knowledge structures called schemata. Learning in this model is the process of adding knowledge to existing structures, slightly modifying the structures, or creating new structures. When new information enters the cognitive system, it is either placed into existing schema, or the schema are slightly modified, or else an entirely new schema is creztod in cases in which new information is discordant with existing information.

There are five common patterns that deal with content learning:

i) Declarative knowledge pattern,
ii) Procedural knowledge pattern,

iii) Structural knowledge pattern,
iv) Extra-instructional pattern,
v) Activity in the environment pattern.

Declarative knowledge pattern: The first type of content learning interaction involves a student message that is declarative knowledge—a statement of fact. This might be in response to a teacher question that has a factual answer, or simply a student expressing what he or she believes to be the truth concerning a situation. A statement of fact is sometimes called a proposition. A proposition has a truth value; that is, a proposition is either true or false. A teacher response could vary from simple knowledge of results all the way through supplying the corrected proposition.

Procedural knowledge pattern: A second type of interaction involves the student's attempt to apply a rule in a new setting—the process of generalisation. In these cases a student is not searching memory for a proposition, but instead is using a form of rule-based knowledge, sometimes called a production system or referred to as procedural knowledge. In these cases, the student message is similar to a hypothesis. That means that there are shades of gray in the way that the rule is applied, and that the "truth" of the behaviour is less clear. Teacher response in these situations needs to go beyond simple knowledge of results or simply telling a student his or her answer is incorrect. The student needs to know why.

Structural knowledge pattern: A third type of student message might be called a statement-of-value that represents one's unique structural knowledge. Within this pattern, each student expresses an opinion on a topic that is expected to be somewhat unique to that student. Often, they represent a complex causal chain of reasoning that is not yet "mature." An example of this type of statement might be, "Women are currently exploiting men in the work force." The response to such a statement might take several forms. The response may simply accept this opinion, in which case an acknowledgement that the message was received might be an appropriate response.

Extra-instructional pattern: A fourth type of mutual coherence could be thought of as a simple request from the student for additional information. The learner requests additional information to be brought into the instructional situation. We would probably see this as a request for clarification.

Activity in the environment pattern: Yet another type of content learning interaction is one of learner activity with the environment. In this pattern of interaction, the learner's "message" is an overt action or a simulation of overt action. The teacher or system response may take one of two forms: it may report back the natural consequences of the act, or it may report enhanced feedback that describes the consequences of the act with more salience.

Affective benefits: The affective benefits of interactivity are less well understood. Interactions in an online classroom provide social presence and satisfaction in mediated situations.

Within a student-entered interaction, there must be some relationship between an entity's message and the response back to that criginating entity. Thus, the analysis of message content should not be made in isolation; the content of both going and returning messages must be considered if we are to make sense of the interaction. We use the term mutual coherence to label the shared meaning between both messages in an interaction. The actual text message that is passed between entities is referred to as the payload. Therefore, we might alternatively define mutual coherence of messages as a sent payload and its response payload that both refer to the same topic.

Most readers have experienced conversations with friends in which our statements are followed by unrelated responses having nothing to do with the topic at hand—almost as if the participants in the conversation are not listening to each other. Most have also experienced the other end of the spectrum, where we have perceived almost a singularity of mind with another human being. In these cases the shared meaning between messages is high; therefore, the mutual coherence is high. Mutual coherence does not address the relationship between the interaction and the goals of instruction. For example, two entities might have a very high mutually coherent interaction that is irrelevant to course goals.

One might suspect that interactions that produce affective benefits are not always directly related to instruction, and in a content learning sense might be deemed irrelevant. However, we believe that these "irrelevant" interactions produce valuable outcomes to the degree that they influence affective benefits.

There are four additional variables that arise through the structural study of interaction. They are:

i) Multiplex messages
ii) Message duration
iii) Information content
iv) Lag time of response.

Multiplex messages: The mechanism by which messages carry information of a cognitive and affective nature is loosely comparable to the manner in which electrical signal components can be combined into an aggregate signal, referred to as multiplexing. In communication lines, there are several mechanisms by which a single line can transmit multiple messages simultaneously. Our analogy is not meant to consider the exact mechanics of the human system, but merely to sketch a similar mechanism for conveying different types of messages with different types of meaning within the same signal. Instructional messages have the potential to carry information concerning both content and affect. In communication theory, the nonverbal components of a message are referred to as paralanguage.

Paralanguage is a powerful mechanism for communicating affect. In distance learning, the term, emoticon has developed to refer to the set of text symbols used to communicate 'emphasis', cynicism and other affective communicative acts. We sometimes fail to notice the dual channel nature of the communication; in written words, paralanguage must be explicitly coded. Purely affective messages are commonly sent between humans in face-to-face communication. The "steely glance" between husband and wife is a classic example of nonverbal communication that conveys displeasure.

In many instructional situations, such as distance learning, Web-based training, or CBT, purely affective messages do not naturally happen in the process. They must be explicitly considered or designed. Moreover, the lack of these affective messages may unintentionally signal lack of interest or lack of caring. Feedback researchers have examined the inconsistency in behavioural theories of feedback that equate feedback as primarily reinforcing with feedback as primarily informational. While they use different terms, the idea that there is a motivational component that is separable from the informational component is a similar idea.

Message duration: Message duration refers to the length of each message in an interactive loop. This variable is operationalised simply as the elapsed time between start and finish of message. Although there are published practical guidelines for message duration, we could find little in the distance education or instructional technology literature explaining this apparently simple variable. We can emphasise the value of this variable by looking at the extreme cases. Consider a course that was extremely transmissive: a 16-week series of videotapes sent to a student with no questions asked during that time. At the end of 16 weeks, the student is required to write a paper that summarised the transmitted data.

The duration of the messages in the interaction are too long, too long, and too short. When we think of interactivity, it is expected that the messages will be of a moderate to short duration. The exact thresholds have not been established, and may be different depending on the situation. At what point does an interaction turn into a series of monologues? There is likely to be an upper and lower range of message duration that defines what most would feel to be an appropriate degree of interaction. However, given the lack of available research in this area, we can only guess that there is an optimal message duration, or that there would be agreement as to what message length constitutes appropriate interactivity.

Amount of information content: The amount of information included in the message and the duration of the messages both contribute to mutual coherence. Amount of information content in this context refers to the amount of new information that is transmitted, independent of the length of the message. A message that we are likely to be able to predict (low entropy) contains less information than a message that is largely unpredictable (higher entropy). The more we know about what message the source will produce, the less uncertainty, the less the entropy, and the less the information. The information content and duration of messages are likely to be the major components of mutual coherence.

Response lag: Response lag refers to the delay between sending an initiating message and receiving a response message in an interactive loop. Response lag can be operationalised as latency between an entity's sending of a message and the eventual time in which the response message returns. In the case of synchronous learning, response lag is usually only a few seconds.

In the distance learning situations that are synchronous in nature, such as interactive television, we would expect to find the same short response lag in many interactions. However, in an asynchronous environment, response lag is expected. In many forms of asynchronous learning, there is a storage medium that maintains messages until they can be read. Using computer networks to deliver text based email (asynchronous communication) generally means that messages will be stored at each entity in the loop.

Distance education adopts many support strategies and uses many support institutions and their infrastructural facilities to maintain a high degree of efficiency and still remain effective. Distance education makes use of many strategies to reduce the gap and to find ways of effectively servicing the students. Anyone professionally involved in education is obliged to presume the existence of two forms of instruction which are strictly separable: traditional face-to-face teaching, based on interpersonal communication and industrialised teaching, which is based on an objectivised, rationalised, technologically produced interaction.

Distance education text, is written specially for the distant learner, sometimes referred to as a teacher in print. It is written with the specific aim of enabling the learner to master a good percentage of the matter, on one's own, and having to rely on the teacher or non-print media, for the rest. It has, therefore, to proceed in large measure as a good teacher would proceed in a normal class, setting learning outcomes for a limited topic of study, asking (intext) questions, summarising, highlighting major or structural concepts, and reviewing the lesson, through a set of questions. Special end-of-despatch questions are also put, and feedback provision made, by giving, the answers on a separate page. A well-prepared print medium accounts for 80-90 per cent or more of the actual learning. However, use of visual m media would have a critical or significant contribution to enhance the quality of learning. For example, in subjects like history, to show a rare document or a monument etc.; in geography and the physical and biological sciences, to show special processes and phenomena, rare species, living or extinct, but of replicas kept in museums or to show a dynamic process or movement etc., or in engineering or for acquisition of practical skills etc. Where the medium also carries a message, awareness cation can be greatly enhanced through the visual medium.

Supportive institutions linking the students with the open school. There may be, in a large system, a number of supportive institutions, set up by the national institution, which in turn, link and are in contact with the study centres. The regional offices would then provide several student services, either directly or through established study centres of the region. Depending on the organisational decisions taken by the national institution, admissions, despatch of study materials etc., and correspondence with individual students may be directly done by the national, office, while the regional office is made responsible for the orientation of teachers/tutors at the study centres and for supervision of conduct of personal contact classes. Another alternative is to decentralise straight from the national institution to the accredited study centres, without having to go through the intermediary of the regional office. Services that the study centres are expected to render would include:

i) Students admission, for, and on behalf of the national office, after students properly fill up the forms, submit the required documents and pay the fees.
ii) Soon after they are admitted to the courses, the services making available to the students, the materials in good

time. Too much delay would result in loss of motivation and would also lead to dropouts.

iii) Distance text is so well written that the student of average ability is able to go through the learning material and master it with only limited additional support. It will mean providing sufficient feedback to the student as he progresses from lesson to lesson or topic to topic, by a variety of techniques, similar to the ones that a good teacher uses in a face to face situation. Thus the distance text is a distant teacher in print. Studies have shown, even where large-scale use of TV and radio support is provided, that the printed distance education text is still the major instrument of learning, accounting for most of it, up to 80 to 90 per cent of it.

iv) The organised provision of personal contact classes, not many in number, but adequate to serve the needs of the students. These contact sessions, to be effective, must be dealt with differently from the way the teacher deals with formal students. Because of the limited number of contact sessions, the methodology will be to enable the student to become a self-learner, to the extent possible. Hence, a survey of the whole course and how the parts hang together is what a good tutor of distance education would begin with. Concept-mapping or mind-mapping is a way of getting the student to get to see and understand the basic structural concepts.

v) Additional support through non-print media. Large-scale use of educational TV is still only a plan and a hope, so is radio, although there are growing provisions being made, especially with the introduction of satellite communication.

vi) Providing institutional facilities for the periodic evaluation of educational attainments. These are of two kinds: one evaluating in the printed study materials, by way of review and to ensure understanding and the other, a more formal internal assessment, marked centrally by the computer, in the national or regional office.

Hence distance education has to make use of the available computer services, for all major aspects: registration and admission of students and creating a student data base; registration of students for internal and external-examinations; computer-marking of some internal assessment tests, correspondence with students, using mailmerge facilities of the computer for personalising correspondence with individual students; print out of mark sheets, certificates and identity cards. Apart from this, the large volume of data on examiners, moderation of examination results, for purposes of scaling and grading, can also optimally use the computer programmes.

Personnel records, financial supervision etc., of the central office can also be assisted by computer programme support, which would then keep and easily retrieve specific data for different categories of users. In fact, once a networked computer system is set up, authorised persons will be able to have access to various kinds of data, in the central computer unit, from a terminal, in their own rooms. Such use can be for decision making or for services to the students, who come asking for information, to obtain the results of an examination or for similar uses.

A careful and discerning simplification has to be made, so that mindless rules, complicated procedures, while retaining proper accountability, do away with cumbersome formalities and filling up of too many unnecessary forms. By evolving permanent dates and calendars, for standard activities, like registration, internal and external examination dates, information and communication become easy and save a great deal of time and cost in terms of postage and telephones.

Decentralisation is not a panacea for dealing with large-size problems and situations, but it offers a necessary strategy. However for its effective use, precautions and fulfilment of certain conditions are equally necessary.

It is necessary that the concerned persons, both staff in national and regional offices as well as partners in the study centres or accredited institutions understand and accept the philosophy and know the procedures. Hence, apart from being efficient and effective, the institution has to become and remain humane and responsive. The demands are so big and challenging, that it is not possible to provide efficiency and effectiveness through the traditional bureaucratic channels of administration.

There has to be, on the ground, real functional autonomy, for purposes of planning, decision-making and implementation. The fact that the finance, whole or part, is coming from the public funds, should not be used as a reason for interfering with the normal functioning of the institution.

Teachers orientation at the study centres is essential. In a large system, training and orientation can be entirely through face-to-face, or through a combination of distance education methods along with some face-to-face or contact classes. Another essential factor is the supervision. But the approach to supervision can also be decentralised and democratised. One key to the success and effectiveness of such decentralised operation is the kind of friendly and on-going academic and administrative supervision that is exercised. Such supervision need not be thought of in the classical, highly stereotyped and bureaucratised fashion. More democratic forms can be evolved. If a cluster of study centres is given the responsibility to supervise themselves and to ensure that all the units of the cluster function well, and asked to organise mutually arranged visits and consultations to meet conditions and norms set by the central institution, that would retain accountability to themselves, to the students and to the central institution, but would also be more human. Obviously, the central institution would also intervene, for orientations and also for visits, but the basic and first responsibility would shift to the members of the cluster.

Another key to success is the actual transfer of necessary authority for decision-making from the central office and a few officers at the top, to the regional office, and to the coordinators at the study centres. The operational strategies of the distance education and the open learning system thus offer an excellent alternative for us to move towards the goal of universalisation of basic education, which is also an essential instrument for human development. There is a close collaboration between the institutions, providing infrastructural and training facilities and the open school, in all aspects, and stages, namely, curriculum development, and the proportionate weightage for the theory practice mix, evaluation and certification. The system of accrediting a course by the open school would enable it to certify the students who pass from a collaborating institution.

The process of accreditation has to be by technical team. Here again, the team must have the basic suppleness to insist on required standards of theory and skill acquisition to meet the demands of the job, without succumbing to the pressures of conforming to an existing formal curriculum. Technologies are developing fast, and unless training keeps these in sight, trained persons will be unfit to meet the demands in the market place.

Hence, updating eduction and training gain importance. The emerging scenario, in a technology-intensive society, will be for more and more trained and skilled manpower. Access to the formal route is difficult, and unnecessarily long, in many cases, apart from having little organised provision for updating or continuing education and training. That is why, the open system must support and complement the formal, by providing both first-time short and longer courses in vocational education, as well as updating and continuing education and training. Continuing education, not necessarily for a certificate, but for life-enrichment, for job satisfaction, or for a variety of life needs, or to pursue an interest or hobby and to acquire various kinds knowledge and skills, whether in citizenship education, legal literacy, health family education, or for personal development and recreation, all offer scope for provision through distance education.

It is possible to teach, in an intellectually honest manner, any topic, to a person of any age. Something similar could be said of distance education, as a medium for providing adequately education in a wide variety of academic and technical skills, if proper links and strategies are ensured. In-service education of teachers, of key persons who work in adult education centres, or health workers and a variety of others, in different development sectors, who need new or continuing education, are some of the other possibilities. The experience of those involved in distance education is that the relative costs are less, and often much less, whether for school level certificate education, or for a course leading to a university degree. This is so, even when large-scale use is made of the electronic media to support print and contact classes.

VIRTUAL TEXTBOOKS

The goal of virtual textbooks is to move learners beyond content mastery to information-seeking and problem-solving skills that include asking appropriate and significant questions of the content; evaluating and synthesising information form diverse sources; understanding and applying the difference between facts and opinions; grasping multiple and diverse perspectives; and drawing insights from these perspectives within the context of one's own knowledge base and experiences.

Physical format of the textbook—with its emphasis on chapters and lessons, done sequentially and linearly—does not easily allow students and teachers to depart from the prescribed path, or to link to new concepts and ideas from other disciplines. Textbooks represent author's views on which information is most important, so the authors' biases are given primary focus. Another key problem facing textbooks is that they become quickly outdated, but revisions take time.

The purpose of virtual textbooks is to construct a learning environment which realises and utilises the web's advantages to the greatest possible extent. The web includes a hypermedia information environment that combines local and distributed course content, instruction, and powerful support utilities in a single integrated problem-centred delivery environment—an on-demand educational delivery system.

In a virtual textbook environment, the teacher can be viewed as a facilitator and need not have full responsibility for knowing all information and delivering it. But the teacher should know how to access the information in a virtual textbook system. Students in a virtual textbook environment are active and interactive learners or problem-solvers. They can work with other students via interpersonal cooperation. Furthermore, in a virtual textbook environment, content has multiple perspectives; information is seen as a vehicle to solve real-world problems; small concepts are taught as variations on larger themes; and insight is valued rather than memorisation of unrelated facts.

Virtual textbooks can be thought of as occupying three concentric circles: (i) problems, (ii) tools, (iii) content. The inner most circle consists of problems that are contextrich, real-world oriented, intrinsically appealing, and increasingly complex. Solving these problems requires the use of various tools and strategies. The outer circle contains content that can be thought of as content-information relevant to the topic of the virtual textbook.

For a virtual textbook to succeed, there must be mutual support and respect between, technical, administrative, and teaching personnel during development of the product. The following four stages constitute a procedure to create virtual textbooks:

i) *Design stage:* During the design stage, planning for course content, objectives, and pedagogy is completed by imagining how the virtual textbook will operate. The teacher must be primarily responsible for this stage and must carefully design how the curriculum and pedagogy are best optimised in this learning environment.

ii) *Development stage:* The development stage involves bringing the design and instructional guidelines onto the computer screen. Technical personnel should handle this stage if the teacher is not competent in the technical aspects, though the teacher must be constantly available for consulting with technical personnel.

iii) *Delivery stage:* The delivery stage begins when the virtual textbook is actually offered to the learning community. The teacher is the primary support for learners during this stage.

iii) *Maintenance stage:* This stage is to enhance the quality of the virtual textbook. The virtual textbook's programmes should be modified by the teacher, technical staff, and students to improve learning convenience and effectiveness.

Relationships among the above four stages are shown in the following figure.

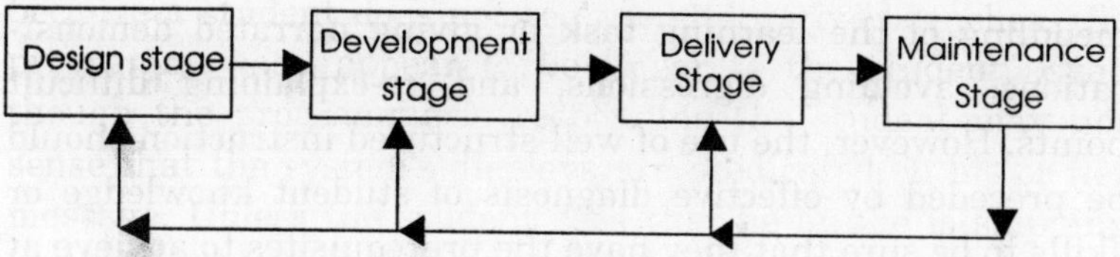

Figure 1: Four stages in developing virtual textbooks

When developing a virtual textbook in Web systems, the following five considerations should be addressed:

i) Pedagogy,
ii) Instructional structure,
iii) Interaction and feedback,
iv) Technology, and
v) Learners' backgrounds.

Pedagogy: The key function of pedagogy is to plan for effective learning. Two general rules in this consideration are: define and describe the purpose of each lesson in the virtual textbook, and define the model of teaching for each goal of each lesson. Virtual textbooks, like traditional textbooks, should be defined according to grade level, subject, and goals. Additionally, any teaching model, based on educational theories such as behaviourism or constructivism, should define the levels of teachercontrol, student-control, and group-control desired regarding each activity or lesson.

Instructional structure: Well-structured instruction provides a step-by-step sequential process and offers systematic and efficient methods to present information. In contrast, ill-structured or loosely structured instruction can operate with messy, ambiguous, and context-sensitive processes of meaning-making. The instruction should be presented in small steps so that one point can-be mastered at a time, providing various examples of the new skills or concepts, meddling of the learning task or giving narrated demonstrations, avoiding digressions, and re-explaining difficult points. However, the use of well-structured instruction should be preceded by effective diagnosis of student knowledge or skills to be sure that they have the prerequisites to achieve at high levels.

The use of ill-structured instruction can help learners develop complex cognitive skills, such as attaining an understanding of important elements of conceptual complexity, the ability to use acquired concepts for reasoning and inference, or the ability to flexibly apply conceptual knowledge to novel situations.

Interaction and feedback: Two general rules in this consideration are: define the level and type of interaction and feedback, and create content and social interaction and feedback in Web systems, the instructional tools include communication and exploration tools. Generally, communication tools, such as e-mail, listservs, chat forums, and computer conferencing, are all appropriate for both asynchronous and synchronous social interaction and feedback.

Exploration tools, such as Web browsers, gophers, and search engines, are all effective for content interaction and feedback. Essentially, interaction is two-way communication among two or more individuals within a learning context, with the purpose either of content completion or social relationship building.

Technology: The virtual textbook should be designed to match participants' comfort with the system and the software. Two general ruler in this consideration are: use the principle of technological minimalism, and provide adequate technical support and training for both learners and teachers. When delivering virtual textbooks, access to often complex and expensive technology becomes a serious issue.

Learners' backgrounds: Web-based environments, unlike structural, computer-assisted instruction (CAI), provide more interactive learning circumstances. Many users of Web systems have found that they could not take advantage of these systems if they lacked the required computer skills, such as experience using database programmes, word processing, and navigating the internet.

Web systems offer the following five characteristics:

i) Web-based systems provide a multimedia environment; information in Web-based systems can be simultaneously represented in any combination of media formats.

ii) Web-based systems integrate various kinds of information and construct information bases; multiple mixed-media nodes in a Web system can be instantly called up in a consistent manner, irrespective of the structure of the information or resources.

iii) Web-based systems support interactive communication; generally, users of the Web have full control over the learning situation, and this high level of interaction gives users dynamic control of information.

iv) Web-based systems support network access to information. A Web-based system goes beyond static Web pages and page linking and can create truly interactive networks with information exchange between users and servers.

v) Web-based systems provide a cross-platform environment; this means that Web systems can be executed independently on various computer operating systems.

REFERENCES

Beare, P.L., "The Comparative Effectiveness of Videotape, Audiotape, and Telelecture in Delivering Continuing Teacher Education, *American Journal of Distance Education*, 3(2), 57-66, 1989.

Bruwelheide, J., "Distance Education: Copyright Issues". In Willis, B. (ed.) *Distance Education Strategies and Tools*, Englewood Cliffs, NJ: Educational Technology Publications, 1994.

Galusha, J. M., *Barriers to Learning in Distance Education, Interpersonal Computing and Technology*, 5(3-4), pp. 6-14, 1998.

Holmberg, B., "Communication in Distance Study", In *Status and trends of Distance Education*, Lund, Sweden: Lector Publishing, 1985.

Jansen, D. G., and Lewis, W. B., "Creating High-levels of Interaction in Distance Education Courses", *ATEA Journal*, 24(1), pp.8-9., 1996.

McHenry, L., and Bozik, M., "Communicating at a Distance: A Study of Interaction in a Distance Education Classroom", *Communication Education*, 44(4), pp. 362-371, 1995.

Oliver, E.L., "Video Tools for Distance Education", In B. Willis (ed.), *Distance Education: Strategies and Tools,* pp. 165-195, Englewood Cliffs, NJ: Educational Technology Publications, 1994.

Verduin, J.R. and Clark, T.A., *Distance Education: The Foundations of Effective Practice*, San Francisco, CA: Jossey-Bass Publishers, 1991.

Willis, B., *Distance Education: A Practical Guide*, Englewood Cliffs, NJ: Educational Technology Publications, 1993.

Wurster, S., *Distance Education: Beneath the Surface*, Techtrends, 1996.

Bibliography

Albrecht, R., Bardsley, G., *Strategic Planning and Academic Planning for Distance Education*, in B. D. Willis (ed.), *Distance Education: Strategies and Tools,* pp. 67-85, Englewood Cliffs: Educational Technology Publications, 1994.

Alcord, B., and Wittgen, A., "The Authority to Think: The Student-centred Classroom", *Contemporary Education*, 61(2), 1990.

Anderson, A H, Newlands, A, Mullin, J, Heming, A. M., Doherty-Sneddon, G and Van der Velden, J., "Impact of Video-mediated Communication on Simulated Service Encounters", *Interacting With Computers*, 8, 2, pp.193-206, 1996.

Anderson, D. T., Garrison, D.R., "Transactional Issues in Distance Education: The Impact of Design in Audioconferencing", *American Journal of Distance Education*, 9, 2, pp. 27-45, 1995.

Aronowitz, S., *The Knowledge Factory: Dismantling the Corporate University and Creating True Higher Learning*, Boston: Beacon, 2000.

Auter, P. I., Hanna, M. S., "The Challenge of Developing Online Courses", *Paper presented at the Annual Meeting of the Speech Communication Association*, San Diego, CA, November 23-26, 1996.

Ackermann, E., *Tools for Teaching: The World Wide Web and a Web Browser*, 1996.

Banathy, B. H., 1968, *Instructional Systems*, Belmont, CA: Fearon Publications.

Barrett M. Sahay S. Walsham G., "Understanding IT and Social Transformation: Development and Illustration of a Conceptual

Scheme", *Proceedings from the 17th International Conference on Information Systems (ICIS'96)*, 1996.

Bauer, J. W., and Rezabek, L. L., 1993, *Effects of Two-way Visual Contact on Verbal Interaction during Face-to-Face and Teleconferenced Instruction*, In *Art, Science, and Visual Literacy: Selected Readings from the Annual Conference of the International Visual Literacy Association*, 24th, Pittsburgh, PA, September 30-October 4, 1992.

Beare, P.L., "The Comparative Effectiveness of Videotape, Audiotape, and Telelecture in Delivering Continuing Teacher Education, *American Journal of Distance Education*, 3(2), 57-66, 1989.

Bell, D., "The Social Framework of the Information Society", In Forester, I (ed.), *The Microelectronics Revolution*, Blackwell, Oxford, 1980.

Bengu G. and W. Swart, A., "Computer-Aided Total Quality Approach to Manufacturing Education in Engineering", *IEEE Transactions on Education*, 39:3, pp. 415-427, 1996.

Bernard, R., and Amundseon, C., "Antecedents to dropout in distance education: does one model fit all?", *Journal of Education*, 4(2), 1989.

Betts, M., "States Bypassing Feds on Information Highways," *Computerworld*, June 20, 1994.

Bichelmeyer, B. A., Kiggins, E.A., "Using Web-based Conferencing in Post-secondary Instruction", *Proceedings of the Annual Conference on Distance Teaching and Learning*, Madison, WI, August 5-7, 1998.

Blanchard, W., *Telecourse Effectiveness: A Research-Review Update*, Olympia, WA: Washington State Board for Community College Education, 1989.

Bricken, M. and Byrne, C. M., "Summer children in virtual reality: a pilot study on educational applications of virtual reality technology", In Wexelblat, A (ed.) *Virtual reality: Applications and Explorations*. Academic, Boston, 1993.

Brooksfield, S.D., *The Skillful Teacher: On Technique, Trust, and Responsiveness in the Classroom*, San Francisco, CA: Jossey-Bass, 1990.

Brown, J. S., Duguid, P., *Learning-in Theory and in Practice*, In J. S. Brown, P. Duguid (eds.), *The Social Life of Information*, Cambridge, MA: Harvard Business School Press, 2000.

Burdea, Grigore and Coiffet, Phillippe, *Virtual Reality Technology*, Wiley-Interscience Publication, 1994.

Brundage, D., Keane, R., and Mackneson, R., "Application of Learning Theory to the Instruction of Adults", In Thelma Barer-Stein and James A. Draper (eds.), *The Craft of Teaching Adults*, pp. 131-144. Toronto, Ontario: Culture Concepts, 1993.

Burge, E., "Adult Distance Learning: Challenges for Contemporary Practice". In Thelma Barer-Stein and James A. Draper (eds.), *The Craft of Teaching Adults,* pp.215-230, Toronto, Ontario: Culture Concepts, 1993.

Burow-Flake, E., Kocher, D., Reiser, A., *Changing Students, Changing Classroom Landscapes: Meeting the Challenge in the Small Liberal Arts Institution,* in L. Lloyd (ed.), *Teaching with Technology, Rethinking Tradition,* Medford, NJ: Information Today, Inc., 2000.

Bruwelheide, J., "Distance Education: Copyright Issues". In Willis, B. (ed.) *Distance Education Strategies and Tools*, Englewood Cliffs, NJ: Educational Technology Publications, 1994.

Carter, A., "Developing Faculty Training for Interactive Distance Education", *Innovations in Education and Training International*, 32(2), 1995.

Chapin, A. L., "The State of the Internet: 1995", *Telecommunications*, Jan. 1995.

Cohen, J. A., Castner, M. H., *Technology and Classroom Design: A Faculty Perspective*, in L. Lloyd (ed.), *Teaching with Technology, Rethinking Tradition*, Medford, NJ: Information Today, Inc., 2000.

Comeaux, P., "The Impact of an Interactive Distance Learning Network on Classroom Communication", *Communication Education*, 41(4), pp. 353-361, 1995.

Cooper R., 'Modernism, Post Modernism and Organisational Analysis 3: The contribution of Jacques Derrida' *Organisational Studies*, EGOS, 1989.

Cromby, J., Standen, P. and Brown, D., "Using Virtual Reality in Special Education", *VR in the Schools,* 1, 3, 14, 1995.

Dalton, D. W., "The Effect of Cooperative Learning Strategies on Achievement and Attitudes during Interactive Video, *Journal of Computer-Based Instruction*, 17(1), 1990.

Dalziel, C., "Copyright, Fair Use, and the Information Superhighway", *Community College Journal*, 1996.

Daniton, Geoffrey and Giacolctto, *Information in the Enterprise: It's more than Technology,* Prentice-Hall of India Pvt. Ltd., New Delhi, 1992.

Dede, C. J., "The Future of Multimedia: Bridging to Virtual Worlds, *Educational Technology*, 1992.

Dick, W., and Carey, L., *The Systematic Design of Instruction* (3rd ed.), Glenview, IL: Scott, Foresman, and Company, 1990.

Doulai, P. and Mandel, M., "Computer and Information Literacy Skills for Professional Engineering Educators", h *the Proceedings of Australasian Universities Power Engineering Conference*, Melbourne, 1996.

Dowe, J., Content-based Retrieval in Multimedia Imaging, *Proc, SPIE Conference on Storage and Retrieval fro Image and Video Databases*, 1993.

Duhaney, D., Technology and the Educational Process: Transforming Classroom Activities, *International Journal of Instructional Media*, 27(1), pp.67-72, 2000.

Duffy, T., Jonassen, D., (eds.), *Constructivism and the Technology of Instruction: A Conversation*, Hillsdale, N., Lawrence Erlbaum Associates, 1992.

Elias N., *The Civilising Process: The History of Manners*, Oxford: Blackwell, 1978.

Ferrington, G. and Loge, K., "Virtual Reality: A New Learning Environment", *The Computing Teacher*, 1992.

Flikner, M., Sawhney H., Niblack W., Ashley J., Huang, Q., Dom, B., Gorkani, M., Hafner J., Lee, D., Petkovic D., Steele D., Yanker P., "Query by Image and Video Content: The QBIC System", in *Intelligent Multimedia Information Retrieval*, Maybury, M.T., (ed.)., American Association for Artificial Intelligence (AAAI), Melno Park, CA, 1997.

Foucault M.,'The Order of Discourse'. The *Rhetorical Tradition*, P. Bizzell and B. Herzberg (eds.) Boston. MA: Bedford Books, 1990.

Forsyth, I., *Teaching and Learning Materials and the Internet* (2nd ed.), London: Kogan Page, 1998.

Gagne, R. M. and Briggs L. J., *Principles of Instructional Design*, Holt, Rinehart and Winston, New York, 1979.

Galbreath, J., "Compressed Digital Videoconferencing", *Educational Technology*, 35(1), 31-38, 1995.

Galusha, J. M., *Barriers to Learning in Distance Education, Interpersonal Computing and Technology*, 5(3-4), pp. 6-14, 1998.

Garrison, D. R., "An Analysis and Evaluation of Audio Teleconferencing to Facilitate Education at a Distance", *The American journal of Distance Education*, 4, pp. 13-24, 1990.

Gevers. T., Smeulders, W.M., "The PicToSeek WWW Image Search System", *Proceedings of the International Conference on Mvltimedia Computing and Systems*, Florence, Italy, 1999.

Graham, S.W., and Wedman, J.F., "Enhancing the Appeal of Teletraining", *Journal of Instructional Psychology*, 16(4), 183-191, 1989.

Guha, A.S., "Student-cetred Open Learning", *University News*, November, 27, 2000.

Harasim, L. (ed.), *Online Education*, New York: Praeger, 1990.

Hawkins, J., "Technology and the Organisation of Schooling (Technology in Education)", *Communication of the ACM*, Vol. 36, May 1993.

Heamshaw, D., "Capitalising on the Strengths and Availability of Desktop Videoconferencing, *Active Learning*, 7, pp. 52-9, 1998.

Hearn G. and Mandeville T., 'The Electronic Superhighway: Increased Commodification or the Democratisation of Leisure?' *Media Information* Australia no. 75, 1995.

Heim, M., *Virtual Realism*, New York: Oxford University Press, 1998.

Henri, F., "Computer Conferencing and Content Analysis", In Kaye, A.R (ed.), *Collaborative Learning through Computer Conferencing*, Springer-Verlag, pp.117-36, 1992.

Hezel Associates, *Educational Telecommunications, State By State Analysis*, Syracuse, NY, 1994.

Hiltz, R. S., *The Virtual Classroom*, Norwood, NJ: Ablex, 1995.

Holmberg, B., "Communication in Distance Study", In *Status and trends of Distance Education*, Lund, Sweden: Lector Publishing, 1985.

Ho, M. S., *Learning and Teaching in Cyberspace: An Empirical Investigation of Computer-assisted Instruction for Geography*, Academic exercise, Dept. of Geography, Faculty of Arts and Social Sciences, National University of Singapore, 1996.

Howell-Richardson, C., Mellar, H., "A Methodology for the Analysis of Patterns of Participation within Computer Communications Courses", *Instructional Science*, 24, 1, pp. 47-69, 1996.

Hudspeth, D. R., and R. G. Brey, *Instructional Telecommunications, Principles and Applications*, New York: Praeger, 1986.

Huges, K., *Entering the World-Wide Web: A Guide to Cyberspace*, Enterprise Integration Technologies, 1994.

Jansen, D. G., and Lewis, W. B., "Creating High-levels of Interaction in Distance Education Courses", *ATEA Journal*, 24(1), pp.8-9., 1996.

Jayanthi Ranjan, Sanjeevi Arul, "Online Teaching", *University News*, 38(3), January, 2001.

Jones B., 'Cultural Maintenance and Change', *Media Information*, Australia. no. 69, 1993.

Jones S., 'Understanding Community in the Information Age' Cybersociety; Computer-Mediated Communication and Community, S.G. Jones (ed) Thousand Oaks CA.: Sage, 1995.

Johnson, D. W., "Student-Student Interaction: The Neglected Variable in Education", *Educational Researcher*, 10(1), pp. 5-10, 1981.

Jorn D., Hill Duin A. and Wahlstrom B., 'Designing and Managing Virtual Learning Communities' *IEEE Transactions of Professional Communication*. 39(4), 1996.

Kearsley, G., "The Nature and Value of Interaction in Distance Learning, In M. Koble (ed.), *The American Centre for the Study of Distance Education Invitational Research Conferencing*

Distance Education: Toward Excellence in Distance Education, University Park, PA: Penn State University, 1995.

Kelch, P. E., Karr-Kidwell, P. J., *How Computer Technology Expands Educational Options: A Rationale, Recommendations and a Pamphlet for Administrators*, ERIC Document Reproduction Service, no. 439 668, 2000.

Kelly, R. V., The end of cognitive Bulimia, *Virtual Reality Special Report,* 3, 1, 38-50, 1996.

Kerr, E. Hiltz, S., *Computer-Based Instruction*, 17(1), 1982.

Khanna S.K., "Challenges of Higher Technical Education in India", *Convocation Address*, DCE, Sept. 1993.

Kirby, E., "Building Interaction in Online and Distance Education Courses", *Paper presented at the Society for Information Technology and Teacher Education International Conference,* 10th, San Antonio, TX, February, 1999.

Kochmer, J., *Internet Passport: Northwestnet's Guide to Our World Online*, Bellevue, WA: NorthWestNet and Northwest Academic Computing Consortium, Inc. (http://info.nwnet.net/passport), 1995.

Kraft. P and Truex D., "Postmodern Management and Information Technology in the Modern Industrial Corporation" R. Baskerville, S. Smithson, O. Ngwenyama and J.I DeGross (eds.) *Transforming Organisations with Information Technology IFIP*, 1994.

Kochmer, J., *Internet Passport: Northwestnet's Guide to our World Online*, Bellevue, WA: NorthWestNet and Northwest Academic Computing Consortium, Inc., (http://info.nwnet.net/passport), 1995.

Kumarasamy, K., Teacher Education in the Twenty First Century, *University News*, November, 27, 2000.

LaQuey, T., *The Internet Companion: A Beginner's Guide to Global Networking*, Reading, MA: Addison-Wesley, 1994.

Li. W., Integrating Image Matching and Classification fro Multimedia Retreival on Web", *Proceedings of the International Conference on Multimedia Computing Systems*, Florence, Italy, 1999.

Loeffler, Carl E. and Anderson, Tim, (ed.), *The Virtual Reality Casebook*. Van Nostrand Reinhold, 1994.

Lochte, R.H., *Interactive Television and Instruction*, Englewood Cliffs, NJ: Educational Technology Publications, 1993.

Maddox, C. C., *The World Wide Web and School Culture: Are they Compatible*?, in D. L. Johnson, C. D. Maddux, and L. Lieu, (eds.), *Using Technology in the Classroom*, New York: The Haworth Press, 1997.

Madhu Parhar, "Surfing Through Web—Exploring a New Educational Resource", *University News*, November, 20, 2000.

Marques O., Furht B., "Issues in Designing Contemporary Video Database Systems", *Proc. IASTED Conference on Internet and Multimedia Systems and Applications,* Nassau, Bahamas, October, 1999.

Martin, B. L., "Using Distance Education to Teach Instructional Design to Preservice Teachers", *Educational Technology*, Vol. XXXIV, No. 3, March 1994.

McHenry, L., and Bozik, M., "Communicating at a Distance: A Study of Interaction in a Distance Education Classroom", *Communication Education*, 44(4), pp. 362-371, 1995.

Meyrowitz. J., *No Sense of Place: The Impact of Electronic Media on Social Behaviour*, New York: Oxford University Press, 1985.

Misanchuk, E.R., "Print Tools in Distance Education", In B. Willis (ed.), *Distance Education: Strategies and Tools,* pp.109-129, Englewood Cliffs, NJ: Educational Technology Publications, 1994.

Minoli, D., *Video Dialtone Technology, Approaches, and Service: Digital and Services: Digital Video over ADSL, HFC, FTTC, and ATM, New York: McGraw-Hill,* 1995.

__________, "Distance Learning Applications, Broadband Networking", *DataPro Report*, 1015BBN, November 1993.

Moore, M.G. and Thompson, M.M., with Quigley, A.B., Clark, G.C., and Goff, G.G., *The Effects of Distance Learning: A Summary of the Literature, Research Monograph no. 2*, University Park, PA: The Pennsylvania State University, American Center for the Study of Distance Education, 1990.

Morgan, A., *Research into Student Learning in Distance Education*, Victoria, Australia: University of South Australia, Underdale, 1991.

Mukherea S., Hirata K., Hara Y., "Towards a Multimedia World Wide Web *Information Retrieval Engine*, http://www.decweb.ethz.ch/.

Newby, G., "Virtual reality", In Williams, M. E. (ed.), *Annual Review of Information Science and Technology*, 1993.

N. Farnes, "Modes of Production: Fordism and Distance Education", *Open Learning*, volume 8, no. 1, 1993.

Oliver, E.L., "Video Tools for Distance Education", In B. Willis (ed.), *Distance Education: Strategies and Tools,* pp. 165-195, Englewood Cliffs, NJ: Educational Technology Publications, 1994.

Osberg, K. M., "Virtual Reality and Education: Where Imagination and Experience Meet", *VR in the Schools*, 1995.

Pantelidis, V. S., "Virtual Reality in the Classroom", *Educational Technology*, 1993.

Paris, S., Turner, J., Situation in Motivation, In *Student Motivation, Cognition and Learning: Essays in honour of Wilbert J McKechie*, P. R. Brown C. E. Weinstein, (eds.), Lawrence Erlbaum Associates, Hillsdale, NJ., 1994.

Paterson K. G. "Student Perceptions of Internet-Based Learning Tools in Environment Engineering Education", *Journal of Engineering Education*, 88:3, pp. 295-304, 1999.

Penny. S., "Virtual Body Building", *Media Information*, Australia no. 69, 1993.

Pentland A., Picard R.W., Sclaroff S., "Photobook: Content-based Manipulation of Image Databases", Chapter 2, *Mutimedia Tools and Applications*, Furht, B.Ed., Kluwer Academic Publishers, Boston, 1996.

Phye, G., "Engaging Technology and Learning Opportunities: Technology Assessment Tools", *Paper presented at the Annual Meeting of the American Educational Research Association*, New Orleans, 2000.

Pimentel, Ken and Teixeira, Kevin, *Virtual Reality: Through the New Looking Glass*, Second Edition. Mc Graw-Hill, Inc., 1995.

Pisapia, J., Coukos, E., Knutson, K., "The Impact of Computer on Teacher Capacity, Attitudes, and Behaviours in Elementary Schools", *Paper presented at the Annual Meeting of the American Educational Research Association*, New Orleans, 2000.

Portway, P., and Lane, C., *Technical Guide to Teleconferencing and Distance Learning.* San Ramon, CA: Applied Business telecommunications, 1992.

Powar, K.B., Quality Assurance in Higher Education, *University News*, November, 27, 2000.

Price, R. and Repman, J., Instructional Design for College-Level Courses Using Interactive Television, *Journal of Educational Technology Systems*, 1995.

Pugliese, R., Telecourse Persistence and Psychological Variables, *The American Journal of Distance Education*, 8(3), 1994.

Reed, J., and Woodruff, M., *Using Compressed Video for Distance Learning*, 1995.

Reid, K. A., *Impact of Technology on learning effectiveness. AT&T CEDL Newsletter,* 1995.

Regan, K., and Tuchman, S., "The Importance of Authority and Peer Relations on the Educational Process of Onsite and Online Communications", *Computers and Education*, 1993.

Savitha Rastogi, "Training of Teachers in Higher Education fro Multicultural Teaching and Learning", *University News*, February , 28, 2000.

Sharma P.B., "Revitalising Technical Education for the New Millennium", *University News*, February 7, 2000.

Sheel Nuna, "Internationalisation of Higher Education", *University News*, February 7, 2000.

Shejawalkar, P.C., Management Education Movement, *University News*, February 7, 2000.

Stenerson, F., "Systems Analysis and Design for a Successful Distance Education Programme Implementation", *Journal of Distance Learning Administration*, 1998.

Stuart, R. and Thomas, J. C., "The Implications of Education in Cyberspace", *Multimedia Review*, 1991.

Tapscott, D., *Growing up Digital: The Rise of the Net Generation*. New York: McGraw-Hill Book Company, 1998.

Turlington, S., *Walking the World Wide Web*, Ventana Press, 1995.

Tiffy J., "The Search for the Virtual Class", *The Virtual University Symposium: A report,* D. Baird (ed.) UltiBASE http://ultibase.rmit.edu.au/Articles/maher1.html, 1996.

Verduin, J.R. and Clark, T.A., *Distance Education: The Foundations of Effective Practice*, San Francisco, CA: Jossey-Bass Publishers, 1991.

Velayo, R. S., "Supplementary Classroom Instruction via Computer Conferencing", *Educational Technology*, 1994.

Wark, M., 'From Fordism to Sonyism: Perverse Readings of the New World Order', *New Formations* 15 Winter, 1991

Watkins, B., and S. Wright, *The Foundations of American Distance Education*, Dubuque, IA: Kendall/Hunt, 1991.

Whitelock D. and Scanlon E., "Motivation, Media and Motion: Reviewing a Computer Supported Collaborative Learning Experience, In *Proceedings of the European Conference on Artificial Intelligence in Education*, P. Brna, a. Paiva and J. Self (eds)., Euro AIED, Lisbon, 1996.

Wileman, R., *Visual Communicating*, Englewood Cliffs, NJ: Educational Technology Publications, 1993.

Willis, B., *Distance Education: A Practical Guide*, Englewood Cliffs, NJ: Educational Technology Publications, 1993.

Williams, M., and Paprock, K., "Instructional Design in Distance Education", *The ED Journal*, 7(4), 1994.

Wilson, A., "Instructional Multimedia in the Math Classroom and Beyond", *Paper presented at the Annual Conference of the American Mathematical Association of Two-year Colleges*, Tulsa, OK, November 3-6, 1994.

Wilson, M. E. and Whitelock, D., "Piloting a New Approach: Making Use of New Technology to Present a Distance Learning Computer Science Course", *Association for learning Technology Journal*, 1996.

Winn, W. and Bricken, W., "Designing Virtual worlds for Use in Mathematics Education: The example of Experiential Algebra, *Educational Technology*, 1992.

Wurster, S., *Distance Education: Beneath the Surface*, Techtrends, 1996.

Yucha, C. 8., Interactive Distance Education: Improvisation helps Bridge the Gap, *Journal of Biocommunication*, 23(1), pp. 2-5, 1996.

Zhao, Z., Cook, J. and Higgen, N., "Online Learning for Design Students", *Association for Learning Technology Journal*, 1996.

Zigerell, J., *The Users of Television in American Higher Education*, New York: Praeger, 1991.

Zhang, S., and Fulford, C., "Are Interaction Time and Psychological Interactivity the Something in the Distance Learning Television Classroom?" *Educational Technology*, 34(6), pp. 58-64, 1994.

Index